1

Devotions for Disciples

- vol. 1

A 120 day guide for meditation and reflection on

God's Word

CHRIST
DISCIPLES
MINISTRIES

Our goal at Christ Disciples Ministries is to equip believers to serve others and fulfill the Great Commission. We do this through pointing our readers in the direction of resources to help them in their personal spiritual growth and by offering daily devotionals.
www.christdisciple.org
www.devotionsfordisciples.com

ISBN-13: 978-0615521992 (Christ Disciples Ministries)

ISBN-10: 0615521991

Preface

It's been my privilege since 2007 to write devotions that are posted on the internet for Christians to meditate and study God's Word in a deeper way. I've tried my hardest over these few years to gain a better understanding of what it is that Christ followers need to be thinking about or what they need to know outside what's talked about in the Sunday sermon. Hopefully the areas I cover are relevant and speak to the needs of the people that read these devotions.

There's nothing more important than what we think about God, or really what we do with what we think about Him. It's so easy to fall into believing doctrines that contradict each other if we don't study God's Word carefully. My aim with Devotions for Disciples is to provide a guide for you do to just that. To study God's Word in a deeper way, to highlight the person of the Holy Spirit (who is far too neglected in many Bible studies), to illuminate the character of Christ (sparking a deeper love for Him), to help you apply doctrine (not just basic beliefs) to your daily walk, and to really think about what it is you believe and why.

I hope you find this helpful as you walk into spiritual maturity. May God bless you richly in Christ.   -Matt Cochran

In the beginning

Genesis 1:1 In the beginning, God created the heavens and the earth.

There was a time before the world existed, before time existed. And yet in that darkness, in that nothingness, there was God. The Triune Godhead of Father, Son and Holy Spirit coexisted even then before there was even such thing as light. And they decided to create.

God created the heavens and the earth, the light, the waters, plants and animals. And it was all good. But something was missing. How could this beautiful creation exist without a master? How could all this be without one who has a soul inhabiting it? And so God created man. But man is unlike any other creation. We're not just some other animal roaming around surviving on instinct. God made us in His image.

The Father, the Son, and the Holy Spirit breathed life into man and he came to be. And it was very good[1]. You and I are God's masterpiece, created in His own image, to bear the identity of the One who made us. We're special to Him. We're created by Him and for Him. And this is where it all begins.

---

1 (Genesis 1:31)

Prepare to meet the Lord

John 1:23 He said, "I am the voice of one crying out in the wilderness, 'Make straight the way of the Lord,' as the prophet Isaiah said."

John the Baptist was well known for baptizing people in water when they confessed their sins and repented. Known to us as the forerunner to the coming Messiah, he was speculated to be many things while he lived on this earth. The thing about John is that he understood his role and never tried to be anything but what God called him to be. He was not the Messiah and he did not try to be even though some thought he was.

The purpose of John's baptism, as he understood it and as we understood it today, was to prepare the hearts of those to whom he preached. You cannot truly be ready to meet the Lord until you've admitted that you need Him.

Repentance means admitting that you're a sinner and therefore that you need God to save you, because the penalty for sin is death[1]. John spoke of making straight the way of the Lord, and part of that is preparing the hearts of the people to receive the coming Christ.

---

1   (Romans 6:23)

Water baptism is symbolic of our death to sin and new life in Christ. John prepared people to meet the Savior before they even knew who He was. This was all ordained by God and worked perfectly into His plan of salvation. Today, we still need to come to Christ, first admitting that we are guilty of sin and incapable of saving ourselves. Only He can save us.

> *"Repentance is more than just sorrow for the past; repentance is a change of mind and heart, a new life of denying self and serving the Savior as king in self's place."*
>
> *-J.I. Packer*

Chosen for holiness

Ephesians 1:4 even as he chose us in him before the foundation of the world, that we should be holy and blameless before him.

What am I here for? What is this life all about? The longer we live, the more we seek meaning in life, the more we may be caught asking these questions. So did God create us with some intent? Did He make each of us with our own purpose? Yes and yes.

Even before time began, when all that existed was God, He thought of you. The Creator chose you in Christ (that is, He chose you to belong to Him as His child) before He even made the earth where you would reside. He made you to be uniquely you, with special talents and abilities – and purpose.

Our purpose on this earth is not to succeed financially and become rich, nor is it to make a name for ourselves and become famous[1]. God made us to be holy and blameless before Him[2]. But how can we achieve this holiness? We can't be good enough to meet God's standards.

---

1   (James 2:5)
2   (1 Thessalonians 4:7)

The Lord planned all along that those He chose would be made holy "in Christ"[1]. We are sanctified and redeemed by the Son of God, and He always intended it this way. Those who are chosen in the Son of God become sons and heirs of God[2].

> *"In holiness God is more clearly seen than in anything else, save in the Person of Christ Jesus the Lord, of whose life such holiness is but a repetition."*
>
> *-Charles Spurgeon*

---

1   (Colossians 1:22)
2   (Galatians 4:7)

Chosen for God's family

Ephesians 1:5-6 In love he predestined us for adoption as sons through Jesus Christ, according to the purpose of his will, to the praise of his glorious grace, with which he has blessed us in the Beloved.

God predestined us for adoption. He chose, before the world even began, to make us sons and daughters. So often we see family terminology used in the Bible to describe our relationship with God. He is our Father, we are heirs, adopted sons. We can't choose our own family members, but God can and did choose His. If you're in Christ, God chose you. You are His and He is yours. And He chose you with a purpose.

God's will is that we would bring Him glory. His main purpose is not merely our redemption but that His holy name would be praised through our redemption. He wants to pour out His goodness and grace on us in Jesus Christ for His glory.

There is nothing quite like the knowledge that you've been chosen by God Almighty to be part of His family to carry out His purpose. But what are you going to do with that knowledge? What will you do with that feeling you get from it? He's equipped you, so what are you doing to act on this fact?

Power in Christ

John 1:12 But to all who did receive him, who believed in his name,
he gave the right to become children of God

One problem we face in the Church today is that many
Christians don't really believe that God can do what He says
He can do. We believe what we read in the Bible, but in
practice, we don't trust God to come through on His promises.
This fear that God won't fulfill his promises is a lack of faith in
the power of God. On one hand, we believe that God can do all
things, and on the other hand when we see situations that look
impossible to conquer, we don't believe He can handle all
things.

Beyond that, we don't believe that we have any power or
authority. The Bible says that to all who received Christ, He
gave power to become children of God. If Christ gave us power,
then we can do all things. Paul said to the Philippians that we
could do all things through Christ who gives us strength[1]. If we
are truly children of God, then we are not impotent, but very
powerful. We have the Creator of all things working through
us.

---

1   (Philippians 4:13)

Don't be afraid to act when God calls you to do something. He won't ask you to do something that He hasn't given you the power to do. If you are called to do it, the Lord will equip you for it. He doesn't call the equipped, He equips the called.

> *"Once more, Never think that you can live to God by your own power or strength; but always look to and rely on him for assistance, yea, for all strength and grace."*
>
> *-David Brainerd*

Redemption in Christ

Ephesians 1:7 In him we have redemption through his blood, the forgiveness of our trespasses, according to the riches of his grace

If someone asked you what it means that we have redemption in Christ through His blood, how would you answer? Dating back to the Old Testament, the understanding of a redeemer was one who ransomed someone else, freed them from slavery or captivity. God was the Redeemer of Israel when He led them out of captivity in Egypt.

You and I have been redeemed too. When we accepted Christ we were freed from the slavery and bondage of sin. We're no longer guilty. Christ's finished work of atonement on the cross through His shed blood ransomed us from sin and we are no longer under its control.

Sometimes we still sin, but it's not because we're under the bondage of sin. We've been redeemed, we're bought and paid for with a price. We belong to Christ. His blood paid our ransom.

His completed work

Philippians 1:6 And I am sure of this, that he who began a good work in you will bring it to completion at the day of Jesus Christ.

The foundation for our spiritual growth is our recognition that our Creator, who began a good work in us through salvation, will bring that work to completion through sanctification. We need to look back at what He's already done so that we can remember how good He's been and keep in mind that He's faithful and will remain active in our lives. We can have confidence that God will never let us go.

Sometimes we need to act on what we know to be true instead of what feels true at any given moment. Feelings are a big part of who we are since we're spiritual beings, but they can often be misleading. When it feels like God isn't living up to His promises, but we know that He's faithful and won't let us go, we need to rely less on feeling and more on what we know to be true.

One way we know that we can rely on God is though His Word. Story after story is documented of His faithfulness to His people. This, along with the evidence in our own stories, gives us hope that He will indeed complete the work that He began.

Blessed for His glory

Ephesians 1:8-10 which he lavished upon us, in all wisdom and insight making known to us the mystery of his will, according to his purpose, which he set forth in Christ as a plan for the fullness of time, to unite all things in him, things in heaven and things on earth.

God loves to bless His people. We don't have to do anything to earn His blessings, they're a free gift – and that includes the gift of His Son. Now lest you get the wrong impression that this is a prosperity gospel message, let's point out that God loves to bless us for the purpose of His glory, not merely for our enjoyment.

He lavished His riches on us in His Son in wisdom – with insight. He chose to reveal Himself to us in the form of Christ Jesus, making known the mystery of His will. He planned this from eternity – it's always been the plan. This revelation brings Him glory and fulfills His will.

It's in Jesus that all things are united. He's the key. He's the deal. In Him all things in heaven and on earth come together. God's plan in showering His blessings on us is to bring glory to Himself and to make Christ known to all. He gives us what we have that He might use us to shine His light.

Our inheritance, and His

Ephesians 1:11-12 In him we have obtained an inheritance, having been predestined according to the purpose of him who works all things according to the counsel of his will, so that we who were the first to hope in Christ might be to the praise of his glory.

We have obtained an inheritance through Christ. We have "been chosen as an inheritance" for Him. In Christ, we receive God as our inheritance and we become His. Our relationship with Him is reconciled in full. Everything that is His, becomes ours, for the glory of God.

What are the implications here? We're in Christ, God is our inheritance and we are His. What does that mean? We get some help with this question from Moses and from Paul. In Deuteronomy 32:9, we learn that God's portion is His people. This passage is speaking of His chosen people, Israel, of the Old Testament. But in Christ even the Gentiles have become God's people[1]. We're in God's family now. We belong to Him as His people.

Romans 8:14-17 explains that we have been given the Holy Spirit and become heirs with Christ. All that is His will be

---

1   (Romans 11:11)

ours as well. The purpose of this, of course, is to bring glory to God. He works all things – our circumstances, our talents, our relationships, our choices – to the purpose of His will. This is what it is to be His and have Him as ours.

We are called to be the praise to God's glory with our lives.

"Blessed be the God and Father of our Lord Jesus Christ, who, according to his abundant mercy, hath begotten me again unto a living hope of an inheritance incorruptible and undefiled, reserved in heaven for me"

-John Wesley

Justified

Romans 8:30 And those whom he predestined he also called, and those whom he called he also justified, and those whom he justified he also glorified.

Justification belongs to those that believe on Christ Jesus for salvation. If you're saved, you were first called, but the thing is, not all who are called receive justification. How is this verse reconciled in light of the fact that not everyone who receives God's invitation to salvation responds to it? The calling here can't refer to the invitation, but must refer to an effective call of the Holy Spirit on the life of the one who would believe and become justified.

You've been chosen with a purpose and with that comes justification. In other words, you've been declared "not guilty" because Jesus took on your sin when He died on the cross. Your sin is forgiven. With that comes a promise.

You'll be glorified on the last day. This is to say that you'll receive a new body, a resurrection body. It'll be perfect, free from all the flaws our current bodies entail. You'll become everything you were created to be, in the image of God. When God called you, He equipped you for faith and He justified you when you followed Christ. This is not without reward. When you get to see Jesus, you'll be justified, sanctified, and glorified.

> *"To be justified means more than to be declared "not guilty." It actually means to be declared righteous before God. It means God has imputed or charged the guilt of our sin to His Son, Jesus Christ, and has imputed or credited Christ's righteousness to us."*
>
> *-Jerry Bridges*

Conformed to His image

Romans 8:28-29 And we know that for those who love God all things work together for good, for those who are called according to his purpose. For those whom he foreknew he also predestined to be conformed to the image of his Son, in order that he might be the firstborn among many brothers.

Romans 8:28 has got to be one of the most quoted and memorized of all Scripture. It's important to know that God purposes all things to work together for good. But when you pay close attention to the latter half of the verse, you see the need to read on.

Paul is stating that there are some who are called by God to fulfill His purpose. In context we learn that those who are called are also to be conformed to the image of Christ[1] in order to bring about that purpose. The work of the Holy Spirit within us brings about our sanctification which numbers us among the brothers/sisters of Christ.

So what's our part in this? What application do we make out of this truth? Trust, for one thing. Do you trust that in all things, in all areas of your life that God is active and present, working

---

1   (see also 2 Thessalonians 2:14)

things towards His purpose? Do you trust that He is conforming you to the image of His Son through the events and circumstances of your life? We've got to trust that, even when things aren't going as we planned, our Creator chose us from before creation[1] to be part of something bigger than ourselves. His plan calls for the lives of His people to be transformed into the image of Christ and He brings that about one step at a time[2].

> "Within each of us exists the image of God, however disfigured and corrupted by sin it may presently be. God is able to recover this image through grace as we are conformed to Christ."
>
> -Alister McGrath

---

1   (Ephesians 1:4)
2   (2 Corinthians 3:18)

That you may obtain the glory of the Lord

2 Thessalonians 2:14 To this he called you through our gospel, so that you may obtain the glory of our Lord Jesus Christ.

He who began a good work in us will see it through to its completion. He's called us not only to salvation but to sanctification. In shaping us and forming us to be more like Christ, God is bringing glory unto Himself.

When we are sanctified through the work of the Holy Spirit we bring glory to Jesus. All glory unto Jesus is also unto the Father[1]. When we are growing into the image of Christ, we desire more and more to do the will of God the Father.

Our part in this, as Paul tells the believers at Thessalonica, is to stand firm. We must hold on to the Gospel which we have been taught because the process of sanctification can be painful. When we face various trials, we need to focus on what God has done and what He will do. It's not only for our own good that He calls us to be made into the image of Christ, it's also for His glory.

---

1   (John 10:30)

Nothing can separate us

Romans 8:35-36 Who shall separate us from the love of Christ? Shall tribulation, or distress, or persecution, or famine, or nakedness, or danger, or sword? As it is written, "For your sake we are being killed all the day long; we are regarded as sheep to be slaughtered."

The life of a Christian isn't without problems, though some expect it to be. The truth is we often find ourselves facing more problems because we're Christians. We might be persecuted, made-fun-of, mistreated, untrusted, or any number of things because we've chosen to follow Christ. Unlike the rest of the world, though, we've got a God on our side who gets us through it all. Nothing can separate us from His love.

Honestly, when we get down to the bottom of why we're attacked at times, it's precisely to try and separate us from God. The insults, the dangers, the threats, they're intended to get us to turn away from Him. Fortunately for us, God is holding onto us tightly through the storms, showing us that He's on our side. What the enemy meant to take us from God will in most cases only serve to draw us closer to Him as we seek shelter in Him. In the trials, His love shows through even more.

More than conquerers

Romans 8:37 No, in all these things we are more than conquerors through him who loved us.

In Christ we will prevail against any attack that comes against us because we are more than conquerors. A conqueror will take on the enemy and claim victory, maybe even winning every battle he ever faces. But one day, like everyone else, he'll die. All of the victories cannot stop death from coming for him. All the battles won will be forgotten.

But in Christ we don't fight temporal battles with little lasting impact. When we fight on God's team we fight eternity-centered battles. Though it may not seem like relying on God to get us through the emotional effects of coworkers insulting us because of our faith could have anything to do with eternity, the underlying truth behind the fact that God is with us in everything we face for His sake is undeniably eternal in nature.

We are more than conquerors because we belong to the One who conquered death itself. We'll live on with Him as victors, having been glorified in Him.

Equipped for service

Ephesians 4:11-13 And he gave the apostles, the prophets, the evangelists, the shepherds and teachers, to equip the saints for the work of ministry, for building up the body of Christ, until we all attain to the unity of the faith and of the knowledge of the Son of God, to mature manhood, to the measure of the stature of the fullness of Christ,

The idea of gifting and that each person has a unique gifting is certainly a familiar one; however, there is a good chance that we need to widen our perspective. Take all of Ephesians 3 and the first section of chapter 4 as your context. Paul describes the radical love of Christ in chapter 3, and then goes on to make several radical statements about how the church is supposed to represent that love. Our lives ought to be worthy of this calling, and it is with that foundation that Christ gifted each of us.

In 4:12, we see the purpose clearly – we have our gifts so that we can be equipped for service, and so that the Body might be built up for Christ's glory. Verse 13 tells us what each man must do. In present day language, it might go something like this:

"Look, each one of you has a skill set. But those skills and gifts are not an end in themselves. We have been called by Christ and given our lives to Him, and our purpose now is to create, in our interactions and daily lives, a picture for the world to see that represents the Love that has been showered on us. Every man must apply himself to growing in Christ. Just as children grow physically, we need to grow spiritually so that each part of the Body is mature and functioning. The people in Ephesus that don't know Jesus, they should be drawn in by their interactions with you, and that will happen when each of us pursues Christ above all else."

Don't be passive. You have certain strengths that will bless other people. Those strengths must be put into action, and they must be under the headship of Christ and used with this over-arching perspective.

Have you ever taken a test to see what your spiritual gifts are? It's a good idea because you can put your gifts to use instead of trying to operate in areas where you may not be best suited to serve. There are lots of spiritual gifting tests online or you can ask your church leadership for their recommendations.

God is on our side

Romans 8:31 What then shall we say to these things? If God is for us, who can be against us?

What's our response to the truth spoken in Romans 8 up to this point? If we know that God has a plan that includes us, that He chose us and called us from before the world's creation, and that He molds us into the image of Christ and justifies us in Him, how can we not trust that He's for us? And if the Almighty Creator of all things is for us, who could possible bring anything up against us that would come even close to matching His might?

If God is sovereign, and by this point in reading Romans you should be able to conclude that He is, then what could ever stop Him? Nothing. And if we're acting on His behalf, carrying out His will, then what could ever stand against us and succeed? Again the answer is nothing.

God is on our side if we're abiding in Him. Nothing stands in our way as we bring about His purpose. Nothing.

He spares nothing

Romans 8:32 He who did not spare his own Son but gave him up for us all, how will he not also with him graciously give us all things?

Are you still in need of convincing that God is on our side? The One who was before all creation cared so much about you and me that He didn't spare His own Son. He could have. The Father could have chosen to keep Jesus in heaven. Who could have questioned Him? He's God! But He sent His real Son in order to give us a chance to become sons through His sacrifice. Does that sound like someone who isn't going to take care of His people?

If He would give us the greatest gift possible to give, why would He not also give us all things through Him? Why would He not meet our needs, not answer our prayers or not stand by us in times of trouble? Our loving God is faithful and stands by His people. He leads us and guides us, provides for us, prepares us and equips us.

Only He satisfies

Psalm 90:14 Satisfy us in the morning with your steadfast love, that we may rejoice and be glad all our days.

Where do you find pleasure? There are so many places in this world to look for fulfillment, but only one satisfies. The things of this world are vain, fleeting, finite, and altogether incapable of filling the void in our lives. They are limited and we're just left wanting more, which leads us to continually search for that "one thing".

The Psalmist knew the key to true joy that satisfies. The Lord's love endures forever, it doesn't fade, it doesn't rust or wear out, it won't leave us. We can be glad all our days if the place we look for fulfillment is in the Lord. In fact, this joy does not have to be sought. It's a byproduct of seeking God first in our lives[1].

When we prioritize God first, He adds to us blessings beyond what we can imagine[2] and the things this world has to offer seem like nothing in comparison.

---

1   (Matthew 6:33)
2   (Ephesians 3:20)

Pray for others

John 17:23 I in them and you in me, that they may become perfectly one, so that the world may know that you sent me and loved them even as you loved me.

Intercessory prayer can be one of the most important acts in the life of a Christ follower. Praying for others is a selfless act of service and one of the greatest things one can do for another person. Even Jesus Himself prayed for others while living here on this earth. Destined to die for the sins of mankind, the Son of God paused in His last few hours on earth and prayed for us.

In John chapter 17, Jesus first prays for His disciples. He asks His Father that the disciples would be sanctified and protected. After this, He prays for all believers who are yet to come. He prayed for our unity, that we would be one. And then, just a short time later, He willingly gave His life on the cross so that we could live. Jesus did not pray that prayer in vain any more than He died in vain. It's His heart's desire that we would be united.

Part of that unity includes praying for each other and

strengthening each other as iron sharpens iron[1]. When we take on each others' burdens, we act in a Christ-like manner, loving our neighbors even as we love ourselves[2]. When we put aside praying for our own desires and needs and pray for those of our family, friends, and even enemies[3], we truly live out our faith in practice. Take time each day to pray for others.

"Our prayer must not be self-centered. It must arise not only because we feel our own need as a burden we must lay upon God, but also because we are so bound up in love for our fellow men that we feel their need as acutely as our own. To make intercession for men is the most powerful and practical way in which we can express our love for them."

-John Calvin

---

1   (Proverbs 27:17)
2   (Mark 12:31)
3   (Matthew 5:44)

That's what friends are for

Hebrews 3:12-13 Take care, brothers, lest there be in any of you an evil, unbelieving heart, leading you to fall away from the living God. But exhort one another every day, as long as it is called "today," that none of you may be hardened by the deceitfulness of sin.

Sin doesn't have to own you and if you're in Christ victory over sin is already yours. The Holy Spirit guides you as you face temptation and provides a way out. But what about that friend of yours who has all the same tools you do but continues to live in bondage to sin?

The writer of Hebrews (apparently a pastor) calls on Christians to lift each other up, to encourage one another. Essentially, he's saying to use teamwork to stay away from sin. Use the buddy system to achieve victory over the evil desires you encounter.

Friends are for a greater purpose than hanging out and having fun. A real friend can stand by your side and encourage you when you're having difficulty with sin and temptation. The Holy Spirit gives you a way out and the friend helps you choose to follow it. You should do the same for them.

Proper motivation

1 Timothy 1:5 The aim of our charge is love that issues from a pure heart and a good conscience and a sincere faith.

In our lives as Christians, we can often get caught up in thinking that we're just supposed to do certain things, obey the rules, and work for God. The problem is that sometimes our motives are all wrong. We do things because we'll be noticed or we do them because we want God to think more highly of us. The Lord, whether we realize it or not, cares very much about our motives. He cares that we do things out of love, a pure heart, and sincere faith.

We shouldn't do things just because we're going through the motions of what we think we're supposed to do and we should never do good things out of selfish motives. A good deed done for personal gain is worth nothing. God's work in us, our sanctification, should lead to fruits that bear witness to Him. Selfish good deeds do no such thing.

Follow the lead of Matthew 5:16 and let your light shine so that others will glorify God because of it.

True security

Psalm 91:2 I will say to the Lord, "My refuge and my fortress, my God, in whom I trust."

Just as we seek satisfaction and pleasure in meaningless things in this life, we also seek security in equally meaningless things. We have a tendency to think that having enough money will keep us safe from disaster or unhappiness, that enough respect will keep us free from loneliness, that enough power will keep us secure from threats.

But the day comes for everyone when that stuff isn't enough. The economy tanks, a mistake is made that ruins a hard-earned reputation, the job that seemed stable is lost. These things, for all they promise, can't provide security. Only he who puts his trust in the Lord will find true refuge.

God is able to be our shelter from life's hurts, our fortress from attack, our deliverer from danger. Only He is enough. Only He can live up to the promise of security. Dwell in Him and He will prove faithful.

Sealed

Ephesians 1:13-14   In him you also, when you heard the word of truth, the gospel of your salvation, and believed in him, were sealed with the promised Holy Spirit, who is the guarantee of our inheritance until we acquire possession of it, to the praise of his glory.

If you are a follower of Jesus Christ, there was some point at which you heard God's Word, felt His prompting, and responded. This might not be an exact moment that you can pinpoint on a calendar, but the fact that there was a period of time over which this process was occurring is certain. God was working in you and you responded to His call. You became part of His family. And He sealed you.

Much like the seal of royalty in times of old, a wax emblem placed on a document so it could only be opened by the rightful recipient, God has placed His seal on us with His Holy Spirit until the right time for our inheritance. No one can snatch us from the Father's hand[1]. He has guaranteed our inheritance as His sons and daughters.

Likewise, in the same way the seal of royalty showed the king's approval of the document (his endorsement), God has stamped

---

1   (John 10:29)

His endorsement on us from the time that we believed on Christ for our salvation. Rest assured. If you are a believer, you belong to the Lord and He belongs to You.

This passage (among others) sometimes opens up the argument over perseverance of the saints, or "once saved, always saved". Regardless of whether one believes that a Christian can walk away from their salvation, most would agree that "no one can snatch us from the Father's hand".

"Don't let obstacles along the road to eternity shake your confidence in God's promise. The Holy Spirit is God's seal that you will arrive."
-David Jeremiah

Protected from evil

Psalm 91:9-10 Because you have made the Lord your dwelling place
— the Most High, who is my refuge— no evil shall be allowed to
befall you, no plague come near your tent.

God's people can be assured that our Lord will provide us with
protection from evil. There is literally no reason to be fearful if
you belong to God in Christ Jesus. Nothing in this world, or in
any world, can stand against Him[1]. No evil can come near us if
we're under His protection.

The Lord will provide His angels to guard us[2], at His
discretion. Nothing can befall us with His knowledge. No
plague, no tribulation, no struggle gets by Him without His
knowledge.

Our God is mighty and able to protect us from all things. He is
our strength and our shield. It's no wonder the words "Fear
not" appear so many times in His Word. If we make Him our
dwelling place, we're safe in His shadow.

---

1   (Romans 8:37-39)
2   (Psalm 91:11)

God with us

John 16:7 Nevertheless, I tell you the truth: it is to your advantage
that I go away, for if I do not go away, the Helper will not come to
you. But if I go, I will send him to you.

Put yourself in the place of the original disciples. You're
walking along daily with Jesus. The Son of God is not only
your teacher, but your friend. You spend time with the one
person on earth who has lived a perfect life and never
committed a single sin. But then, just when you think things
are going great, He tells you He's going to go away. He's going
to die. What do you do with that?

We can't blame Peter for his reaction to Jesus's news. When he
swore it couldn't be so, Jesus rebuked him and we, living so far
removed from that moment, are quick to judge his stupidity.
But let's be honest, we would most likely have done the same
thing Peter did. If Jesus lived right here among us, if we
thought He was going to establish His kingdom right here and
now, we'd have tried to keep Him around too. But Jesus
pointed out that it was actually to our advantage that He go
away. How can this be?

When Christ came to earth as a man, He emptied Himself of

His divine prerogative. He, as a human man, could only be in one place at a time. In the brief time He was here in the flesh, He could not be omnipresent. He could not be with every single person at once. But by sending the Holy Spirit (who, by the way, operated in Christ at all times), we could have God present with us always. If God was still present in the form of Jesus in a historic place and time, we wouldn't be able to experience His divine guidance unless we were right there with Him. But the Holy Spirit is our helper whenever and wherever. His power operates in us and through us to the glory of God.

> "When God spoke to Moses and others in the Old Testament, those events were encounters with God. An encounter with Jesus was an encounter with God for the disciples. In the same way an encounter with the Holy Spirit is an encounter with God for you."
>
> -Henry Blackaby

Conviction by the Spirit

John 16:8-11 And when he comes, he will convict the world concerning sin and righteousness and judgment: concerning sin, because they do not believe in me; concerning righteousness, because I go to the Father, and you will see me no longer; concerning judgment, because the ruler of this world is judged.

What is the Holy Spirit? Is it a force? Something that makes people act crazy in church? Maybe it's our conscience. A ghost? What is the purpose of the Holy Spirit? What does the Bible say?

First, the point must be made that the Holy Spirit is not an "it", but a "He", the third distinct person of the Trinity. The Holy Spirit is God, just as Jesus is God and the Father is God. His purpose is unique and He moves in the lives of people to make things happen. Jesus spoke of the Holy Spirit when He was about to ascend back into heaven. He pointed out that once He was gone we'd still have God with us because we'd be given the Spirit. But so few of us understand what this means.

If you're a believer, it's only because you were first called by the Holy Spirit. God was working in your life to reconcile you to a right relationship with Him. You and I don't have it in us to move towards God without Him initiating. Our sinful nature makes us want to move away from God, not towards Him.

The Spirit convicts the world of sin[1], of judgment[2], and of righteousness[3]. Jesus no longer walks among us as our example for what righteousness and holiness are, so the Holy Spirit's job is to reveal them to us. It's also His job to reveal God's character to other people through us by enabling us to show the Fruit of the Spirit. Lives are changed by the work of the Holy Spirit, who glorifies Jesus.

---

1   (makes us aware of our sinful nature and need for forgiveness)
2   (to show us the penalty that has to be paid for our sin)
3   (to show us the character of God and all that's good)

The Spirit declares

John 16:13-14 When the Spirit of truth comes, he will guide you into all the truth, for he will not speak on his own authority, but whatever he hears he will speak, and he will declare to you the things that are to come. He will glorify me, for he will take what is mine and declare it to you.

In moments where something spiritual that once seemed unclear becomes clear, the Holy Spirit is at work. Whether it's a verse of Scripture or something you're learning through prayer, God is working in you for the purpose of His own glory. When we need an answer from God, it's not often that we'd hear an audible voice speak to us. It's more likely that we'd "hear" from Him through the person of the Holy Spirit.

The Spirit guides us in truth. He helps us discern right from wrong, allows us to see what sound biblical doctrine looks like, He declares to us what God is revealing. When we're in need of direction, it's the Holy Spirit that shows us the way. When we're looking for God's will, it becomes clear[1] by way of the Holy Spirit's work. He convicts us of sin, leads us in truth, and speaks to us the things of God.

---

1   (though usually not all at once)

It's because of the Holy Spirit that we're able to bring glory to God. He molds us and shapes us to be of godly character, bearing witness to Christ through our example to others. He loves others through us, accomplishes the Father's will through us, and empowers us. He's God in us and He's what other people see of God through us.

The promise

Luke 24:49 And behold, I am sending the promise of my Father upon you. But stay in the city until you are clothed with power from on high.

Before Jesus departed from His disciples to be with His Father, He relayed to them a promise. This promise caused their entire lives to change. These ordinary fishermen, tax collectors, and otherwise nobodies took part in the birth of a movement that would turn the world upside down. That is, after the promise, and after they waited for it.

When Jesus gave His followers the Great Commission in Matthew 28:18-20, He didn't send them out alone to accomplish His will. He told them that with his departure would come another. The Holy Spirit would be poured out on them, just as promised, and they would receive power from God to do everything they needed to do to bring about His purposes. The power of the Holy Spirit changed them from cowards who ran at the time of Jesus' arrest and trials to bold evangelists who proclaimed the Gospel to thousands upon thousands.

They waited for this power because they knew Jesus was true to His word. The man who predicted that He would rise from the dead had more than earned their trust. They knew the power would come and they knew when He showed up. There was no reason left to question, only reason to act. And the Holy Spirit helped them to do that too.

Pentecost

Acts 2:38 And Peter said to them, "Repent and be baptized every one of you in the name of Jesus Christ for the forgiveness of your sins, and you will receive the gift of the Holy Spirit.

In Christ, the many promises of God to His people, the Jews, came to pass. He encompassed all that God had chosen to reveal to man. In the Holy Spirit then, all of the promises of Christ to His people, the Christians, were fulfilled. Jesus had told His followers to go and wait for Him after He had resurrected and reappeared to them. He promised if they waited they would receive power.

And so they waited. They hid, really. They were all together in one place on that day, the day of Pentecost. And when they received the Holy Spirit they all were given the power to speak in languages they didn't know, for the purpose of evangelizing to others in his/her own tongue. Those who heard them were amazed that these uneducated men were able to speak many languages. Some scoffed, some mocked...but they listened.

As they listened, the previously timid disciples who were in hiding boldly came out among them and preached the gospel. Peter delivered a sermon that brought around 3,000 to Christ that day. It wasn't a "here's how to get a better life" sermon, or even a "Jesus loves you" speech. Peter simply pointed to the truth through events that had taken place and then let the conviction of the Holy Spirit do its work in the hearts of the people. They heard it and were "cut to the heart"[1]. Then Peter gave them a chance to respond, which they did.

The work of the Holy Spirit in believers on Pentecost is the same power He employs today in us. Things may not always be so drastic as to see thousands of people saved in one moment, but His conviction in their hearts and His work in us to be bold in speaking the truth is still very real, just as it was for Peter and the eleven. He may not ever urge you to speak in tongues or to preach in front of a massive crowd, but He will empower you to do God's will in whatever situation you do find yourself in.

To God be the glory.

---

1   (Acts 2:37)

The Spirit as a guarantee

2 Corinthians 1:21-22 And it is God who establishes us with you in Christ, and has anointed us, and who has also put his seal on us and given us his Spirit in our hearts as a guarantee.

Paul wrote once about his ability to be content in all situations. How is it that he was capable of such a steady demeanor, regardless of whether he was in prison or in comfort? A statement in his second letter to the Corinthians gives some good insight. He writes to them after his plans changed and he was not able to visit as he would have liked to. His attitude though is one that shows full trust in God. He speaks of active ongoing action on God's part[1], completed action[2], and the guarantee that God has given.

Paul could be content because he knew that no matter where he ended up God had sent him. When he was sent, God equipped him. And when he went, God protected him. He knew the Lord was with him at all times because he had been given the Holy Spirit as a guarantee. So have we. God is with us at all times because, as Christians, we are inhabited by the Holy Spirit. He lives in us and works through us. We are

---

1   (establishes us)
2   (anointed us)

sealed as God's own by His Holy Spirit in us.

The Holy Spirit can do great things through us, and that includes granting us boldness to speak the truth and courage because we know we are guaranteed His presence no matter where we are. We're never without God because He establishes us, equips us, and seals us.

An aroma

2 Corinthians 2:15-16 For we are the aroma of Christ to God among those who are being saved and among those who are perishing, to one a fragrance from death to death, to the other a fragrance from life to life. Who is sufficient for these things?

As followers of Christ, we represent the Lord whether for good or for bad. What we say and do can have an impact on the faith of other people because we're agents of God, and for some, the only thing they'll know of the gospel. But truth be told, sometimes when we're at our best, that is, most rightly representing Jesus, people will hate us. Some people will hate us, not because of something we did wrong, but because of something right in us. Some people are repelled by the aroma of Christ.

Some will experience the gospel message through us and turn to God, others will sense the gospel message in us and turn away. The thing is, it's not our job to make sure that every person gets just the right scent, it's our job to represent Christ in all we say and do. Some people will be turned off from this, and there's nothing we can do about it.

We do none of this on our own. The responsibility of being a representation of Christ is huge and we just aren't sufficient in our own strength to carry that out. The Holy Spirit works in us to make sure that those who will turn to Him see what they need to see.

You never know who's watching you and basing their view of God on what they see. Fair or not, it's our duty to always be on the path God has for us so that other people can see His love and come to know Him.

Letters from Jesus

2 Corinthians 3:3 And you show that you are a letter from Christ delivered by us, written not with ink but with the Spirit of the living God, not on tablets of stone but on tablets of human hearts.

We may not always realize the impact our lives have on those of others, but it's a significant matter. Our experiences with other people can change the way they think or feel about any number of subjects, including God. How we represent Christ can make a difference in the way others see Him.

Jesus was sent to this earth as a self-revelation from God. In Him we see all of the attributes of God in human flesh. He walked the earth and those who lived during that time saw God for what He is. Now, Jesus ascended back to sit at the right hand of the Father in heaven, so who is left to represent God?

The Holy Spirit was sent to do God's work in and through us as Christ followers. Now, we are God's letters written to human hearts. We are what people look on and see God's character[1]. The Holy Spirit connects our hearts with those of others, helping us bear witness to the work of Jesus and His saving grace. At times it may not even be something we say or do that

---

1   (although not perfectly as in the person of Christ)

draws another to Christ. It may seem unexplainable how they came to know the Lord through us, but that's all the more proof that it's Him doing the work.

Ministers of a new covenant

2 Corinthians 3:6 who has made us competent to be ministers of a new covenant, not of the letter but of the Spirit. For the letter kills, but the Spirit gives life.

Trying to keep up with every rule and restriction can be tiresome and in the end doesn't bring about perfection anyway. We're unable to keep the whole law and that's why we have it. The law shows us that we are imperfect and in need of a savior. In Christ we have that Savior and a new covenant, one not dependent on rule-keeping, but on grace.

Trying to reconcile with God based on following the rules and doing good will still result in death. We cant' reach God in this way. Only through the grace of Christ do we have a chance at a right relationship with God. Now He's made us ministers of that new covenant. He's shown us grace and now we're to show grace on His behalf.

The Holy Spirit works in us to show the life-giving grace of God to others through our lives. Because we've been forgiven, we are empowered to forgive. Because we've been shown love, we are able to show love. Only with the help of the Holy Spirit are we competent to minister to others in this way.

The Spirit gives freedom

2 Corinthians 3:17 Now the Lord is the Spirit, and where the Spirit of the Lord is, there is freedom.

The law brings bondage. Rule-keeping is grueling and not productive. Real freedom doesn't come from doing what the law says, but from God. He has set us free by His grace and forgiveness.

We can search around for peace and joy and happiness, but we'll only find them in Christ because only His completed work on the cross can bring us the forgiveness we so desperately need. The Holy Spirit works in us to bring about contentment and joy and they're only accessible because Jesus chose to come to the earth and take on our sin and put His righteousness onto us. This is why we are free, we have the righteousness of Christ.

God looks down on us and sees His sons and daughters and not the sinners that we are because we're clothed in Christ. Freedom is experiencing God's love in Christ. The Holy Spirit enables us to experience it.

The fruit of the Spirit – Love

Galatians 5:22 But the fruit of the spirit is love…

Paul starts out the portion of his letter to the Galatian
Christians on the fruit of the spirit by stating that love is one of
the quality traits we should bear as followers of Christ. One
should think there is no coincidence in the fact that this is the
first trait listed in the fruit of the spirit. Love is a major theme
in God's Word.

Why is it that love is so important in the life of a Christ
follower? Why would love be so important to be listed first
among the fruit of the spirit, mentioned so many times
throughout the scriptures, and spoken of so often by Jesus
Himself? Because without love, everything else is worthless.

Many wedding ceremonies include a reading from I
Corinthians 13. We call it "the love chapter". A wonderful
chapter it is, but we often hear it quoted starting in verse 4.
This is where the characteristics of love are given. Look just
before that verse to find what Paul says on the importance of
love. "…if I have all faith, so as to remove mountains, but have
not love, I am nothing. If I give away all I have, and if I deliver

my body to be burned; but have not love, I gain nothing."[1]

Did you catch that? If we have the faith to move mountains, but don't have love in our hearts, it's worthless faith! All too often we place more importance on faith and works than on love. The fact is, that those works and that faith ought to be based in love. When we perform kind acts, it should be out of love, not duty. When we sing songs of praise to the Lord, it must be out of love for Him, not obligation.

When Jesus Christ was questioned as to the greatest of the commandments, He listed near the top "love your neighbor as yourself"[2]. If we can keep this commandment, almost everything else we're instructed to do will come as a natural byproduct.

> *Love is helping people toward the greatest beauty and the highest value and the deepest satisfaction and the most lasting joy and the biggest reward and the most wonderful friendship and the most overwhelming worship -- love is helping people toward God. "*
>
> *-John Piper*

1   (2b-3)
2   (Matthew 22:39)

The fruit of the Spirit – Joy

Galatians 5:22 But the fruit of the spirit is…joy

What's the first thing that the nonbeliever can see about a professed believer? It could be argued that one's emotional state is the first impression that an observer can pick up. If we, as Christ followers, have no joy we don't send a very appealing message to those watching. If we are to convince the unsaved that we have something that they should want, we should act like it.

This is not to say that we should, at all times, have an ear-to-ear grin on our faces. Times will come in our lives that are nothing to smile about. But if we have the joy of Christ inside us, the way we handle the bad times will be different than the way someone who doesn't have Christ would handle them. We can show that we have an overall joy in our lives even as we go through down times in our lives. It's in these times that we will be watched the most.

It can be quite easy to put on a happy face and act like life is perfect even though we know it isn't, but real joy isn't about putting on a facade to fool everyone. The Lord's instructions are not to fool anyone. It is about living out the joy that is

within us. Look to Christ as an example.
[1]

"Joy is the serious business of Heaven."

-C.S. Lewis

---

1   See also Matthew 6:27, John 15:11, John 10:10, Romans
     8:35, 2 Corinthians 4:9, Psalm 5:11, Psalm 28:7.

The fruit of the Spirit – Peace

Galatians 5:22 But the fruit of the spirit is…peace

Love…joy…and now peace. The fruit of the spirit begins with three very related attributes that a Christ follower should exemplify. Related because the first leads to the second, and the second leads to the third. Without love, we would have no joy; and with no joy, we could have no peace. This means that, indirectly and directly, we cannot have peace without love.

Peace is a byproduct. If one merely strives for peace, but does not achieve the other fruit of the Spirit, peace will not be reached. Much the same can be said for the remainder of the fruit. And it all starts with love.

Peace can be a very elusive thing in our time. With our world constantly growing more busy, one can barely find the time to think about peace, let alone obtain it. It doesn't help that we're told from every source around us that we should only look out for ourselves and our own pleasure. The lie of the world is that we will gain peace by seeking the things of this world and thinking only of selfish ambition. But peace will never be reached in this way.

True peace, the kind that Christ promises, cannot be caught by trying to catch peace. No, it is a byproduct of a Christ-centered attitude and heart. When we follow after the will of God, when we love others, when we help those in need, when we exemplify love and have joy, we will get peace. The peace that transcends all understanding[1] will be ours if we seek the Lord first and foremost in our lives.

> "A great many people are trying to make peace, but that has already been done. God has not left it for us to do; all we have to do is enter into it."
>
> -Dwight L. Moody

---

1   (Philippians 4:7)

The fruit of the Spirit – Patience

Galatians 5:22 But the fruit of the spirit is…patience

Patience is never a subject that Christians want to hear a message about. We've all experienced praying for patience, only to have the worst day ever. This may be where the saying "Be careful what you wish for" came from. It seems that when we pray for patience, the Lord gives us some training.

But we should all strive to show patience, so that others may see that something different in us. We must be the ones in the frustrating situation who are keeping a cool head. This is an open door to witnessing to nonbelievers. When we keep our cool, even though everyone around us is losing theirs, people may ask us how it's so. We must walk through that open door.

If we are to bear fruit as a witness to our Savior, we must have patience to deal with all things that come our way. If we do not have patience with nonbelievers, we will not show them love. If we do not have patience, we will not show kindness in a world that lacks it. Without patience, there is no self-control, and so on and so forth.

To bear any fruit of the spirit, we must exercise patience.

The fruit of the Spirit – Kindness

Galatians 5:22 But the fruit of the spirit is…kindness

Kindness is hard to come by in today's society. Even kind acts are sometimes done out of selfish motives. But if we are to truly bear the fruit that God has in mind, we must act in kindness out of love, not out of selfish ambition. Our motives matter a lot to God.

It's true, that we are often rewarded for our kindness in this life. This, however, should not be our objective in doing kind things for others. Our main focus is to bring glory to God through our actions. Whether that is helping the poor, tutoring children, reading to our own kids, or whatever.

Kindness, again like so many attribute of the fruit of the spirit, comes out of love and it related to the other fruit. Without joy, we will not be able to show kindness because we will not be in the right state to do so. Without patience we will never be able to show kindness because sometimes we're required to show kindness to those that are hard to love.

Show kindness from your heart, and show the love of God the Father to those who don't know Him.

The fruit of the Spirit – Goodness

Galatians 5:22 But the fruit of the spirit is…goodness

The Christian faith is one that is plagued with a sometimes unflattering past. The view that nonbelievers take of the religion to which we belong is not always a positive one. Despite our best efforts to put forth a good face to Christianity, some will focus on the negative events that have taken place in history.

This is all the more reason why we, as Christ followers, should put forth the very best example at all times. In all that we do, we need to show goodness. When we are wronged, we need to react, not with more wrong, but with good.

We need to be using our time to help the poor, the widows, and the orphans. Wherever there is need, it is those who follow Christ and do His will that should be at the forefront of the effort to bring good to the situation.

And in all these things, it is not our effort that brings about good. It is the Holy Spirit in us that bears this fruit for all to see.

The fruit of the Spirit – Faithfulness

Galatians 5:22 But the fruit of the spirit is…faithfulness

Our main goal as followers of Christ should be to act with the character of Jesus, our Savior. There is no better way to lead others to Him than to show them exactly who Christ is. Words make a huge impact, but nothing can compare with the example we set through our actions.

In His earthly ministry, we see that Jesus was always faithful. There is never a time that our Lord makes a promise that He does not fulfill. We also should strive for this quality. We should be faithful in all we do.

In this world filled with so many excuses to get out of everything from paying what we owe on debt to facing the consequences of sin, it takes little effort from us to be unreliable. But as Christians, we are to set the example of what faithfulness means.

Faithfulness in our jobs means putting in a full day's work for a full day's pay. Faithfulness in our marriage means remaining true to our vows, keeping ourselves pure, not only physically by mentally as well. Faithfulness to our children means not making promises that we don't intend to keep.

And, just as important as those examples is our faithfulness in areas that can be seen in public by nonbelievers. The world must see us living the qualities we profess to believe in. Making excuses is not Christlike. Ask the Holy Spirit to bear this fruit in your life for all to see, for it brings glory to God.

"Love, joy, peace, patience, kindness, goodness, faithfulness, gentleness, and self-control. To these I commit my day."

-Max Lucado

The fruit of the Spirit – Gentleness

Galatians 5:22-23 But the fruit of the spirit is...gentleness

How are we to react to the aggravating situations that we
sometimes face in life? Now answer the question how do we
react in those situations. The answers often do not line up with
each other.

Using Jesus as an example[1], we should always treat others with
gentleness. We've spoken of kindness, and this differs just
slightly. While kindness is more of a way of acting, gentleness
brings up more of an idea of a state of spiritual being. While
one acts in kindness, one is of gentle spirit.

We are told that "A gentle answer turns away wrath, but a harsh
word stirs up anger" in Proverbs 15:1, to "Be completely
humble and gentle; be patient, bearing with one another in
love" in Ephesians 4:2, and also to"Let your gentleness be
evident to all. The Lord is near" in Philippians 4:5. Our
instructions are clear. Be gentle, not harsh. Speak words of
love, not hate.

We can bear this fruit through the Holy Spirit living inside of

---

1   (Matthew 11:29)

us. And we should let it show to all the world to bring glory to God and to fulfill His will.

> "*Gentleness is an active trait, describing the manner in which we should treat others. Meekness is a passive trait, describing the proper Christian response when others mistreat us.*"
>
> *-Jerry Bridges*

The fruit of the Spirit – Self-control

Galatians 5:22-23 But the fruit of the spirit is…self-control

"I can't believe I did it again." How many times have we all found ourselves in the situation that leads to such a thought? We tried to control ourselves, but that one thing that just always seems to creep back into our lives overtook our willpower once again. Yes, we gave in to temptation.

It's a likely scenario, both for the nonbeliever and the Christ follower. It can be very difficult to keep our fleshly urges under control, whether those urges are overeating, lusting, drinking heavily, cheating, stealing, lying, or any other number of sins. The difference between us and those who are not redeemed by the blood of Christ through accepting His gift of salvation, is that we have been granted power above what we are humanly capable of possessing. We are not impotent to change our situation. We have the Holy Spirit working in us.

In the matter of self-control, the name given to this trait referenced in the Fruit of the Spirit scripture may be a bit of a misnomer. For it is not really "self" control that we possess, so much as it is "Spirit-control". We have been given the ability to restrain ourselves through the help of the Holy Spirit living within us, as believers. We are told in Paul's first letter to the Corinthians that "No temptation has seized you except what is common to man. And God is faithful; he will not let you be tempted beyond what you can bear. But when you are tempted, he will also provide a way out so that you can stand up under it." That one passage is reason enough to believe that we are quite capable of bearing the fruit of self-control in our lives.

Self-control is not about trying our hardest not to sin. Rather, self-control, like the other Fruit of the Spirit, is attained through submission of our lives to the leading of the Holy Spirit.

From one degree of glory to another

2 Corinthians 3:18 And we all, with unveiled face, beholding the glory of the Lord, are being transformed into the same image from one degree of glory to another. For this comes from the Lord who is the Spirit.

You are not who you once were. You're not who you were before Christ, but you're also not who you were right at the moment He entered your life. You're being transformed by God to be more like Him. He's revealing more of Himself to you and as He does that, you gain more of His character. To know Him is to behold Him.

Change doesn't happen overnight. No, each and every thing that God needs to work on in your life to give you the image of Christ is done one bit at a time. One event at a time. One circumstance at a time. One tragedy at a time. One triumph. One stint of suffering. All of it, everything that happens in your life is part of the process. It may not seem so now, but over time it will make more sense. Look back at where you were and where you are now. Think of all the things you've been through that have shaped you into what you've become. And the process is only just beginning.

The journey of sanctification is ongoing and doesn't stop until we're just like Christ. It won't end in this lifetime, but it will have an impact here. As the Holy Spirit works in you, it affects your character and the fruit you bear as a Christ follower. You walk more closely with God, understanding more as He reveals more of Himself. God is glorified in you and through you.

I must have read this verse dozens of times before it really meant anything to me. Then one day it hit me like a ton of bricks. Ever since that day, I can't get away from the beauty of this passage and all it means for my life.

The light of the gospel

2 Corinthians 4:6 For God, who said, "Let light shine out of darkness," has shone in our hearts to give the light of the knowledge of the glory of God in the face of Jesus Christ.

How does God reveal Himself to us? Many have asked this question and many will continue long after we're gone from this earth, but the answer has been given. God revealed Himself in the form of Jesus, who walked the earth among men, facing our temptations and yet never giving in to them, living a perfect life in perfect harmony with the Father. In Christ, the character of God was revealed and lived out. And in God's Word, Jesus is revealed to us who never got to walk in His presence on earth.

But to some the gospel is nonsense, they can't make anything of it. They've been blinded to the power of the gospel as though they're in darkness. But to those of us whom God has called, to those of us who have responded, He has shone a light. He has illuminated Jesus in the gospel to show us the glory of God, and He's done it in our own hearts.

Apart from God working in us, we can't understand His revelation, we can't see Jesus for who He is. But when God gives the light, we can see everything for what it is. His truth is made real, His character is made clear. Then and only then can we begin to know Him.

> "The Spirit inspired the Word and therefore He goes where the Word goes. The more of God's Word you know and love, the more of God's Spirit you will experience."
>
> -John Piper

Jars of clay

2 Corinthians 4:7 But we have this treasure in jars of clay, to show that the surpassing power belongs to God and not to us.

We're here and then we're gone. So short are these lives we live on earth, but we seem to think we've got forever. We think that we can solve all of the world's problems, if only given enough time. But none of us has that kind of time. It was designed that way. We're here, and then we're gone.

We weren't made to live in these bodies forever, they're our temporary homes. We give witness to the death of Christ through the death of our own bodies, but our spirits live on and bear witness to His resurrection with our own resurrection. We depart these jars of clay and trade them in for the real vessels our souls belong in.

To some, death is a terrifying, sad thought. But to those of us who belong to Christ, it's only the beginning. Our knowledge, our strength, our capacity to love, all of these things are limited here on earth, in these bodies. What God has in store far surpasses anything we know here. This is just a warm up for the main event!

Afflicted, but victorious

2 Corinthians 4:8-9 We are afflicted in every way, but not crushed; perplexed, but not driven to despair; persecuted, but not forsaken; struck down, but not destroyed;

We face all sorts of opposition in this life, both before and after our conversion and rebirth in Christ. As we journey down the road of discipleship we'll meet lots of challenges along the way, but they can be used to build us up instead of destroying us. With God on our side, we will be victorious.

As followers of Jesus, we don't operate in our own strength, we have the Creator by our side. His strength is made perfect in our weakness[1]. His power shows through when we have none. When we embrace our weakness and rest in Him, His power shows in us. When we're weak, then we're strong[2].

It's for the sake of Christ that we endure all this life has to throw at us. It's so His power can be made known, so His strength can be evident in our lives. We're given over to death in this body so that His life can be made real in us for all to see. It's for His glory that we face trials, and just as we die like

---

1   (2 Corinthians 12:9)
2   (2 Corinthians 12:10)

Christ we'll be resurrected and glorified. He was victorious over death, so now we can be too.

While it may be difficult during hard times to keep this promise in mind, holding onto this and clinging to it can get you through anything.

Preparing for glory

2 Corinthians 4:17 For this light momentary affliction is preparing
for us an eternal weight of glory beyond all comparison,

From the day we're born, we're dying. We grow, we learn, we
love, we laugh, we experience all of the things life has to offer.
But we all reach and end to this life. Praise be to God that this
life is not all there is! We have something wonderful to look
forward to – life eternal. This life is momentary, but the life
after this one is never-ending.

All of the hardships we face here, they're building us up,
conforming us into the image of Christ, from one degree of
glory to another. Sanctification takes place in this life, the Holy
Spirit doing His work in us to make us what God intended us
to be. We endure all that there is here for the reward we
receive later when sanctification ends and glorification begins.

We carry with us the death of Christ. We die as a reminder
both of the fact that sin brought death into the world and a
testimony to the fact that Jesus saved us from eternal death.
We live forever with Him because of what He did on the cross.
His death spared us ours. His resurrection gave us a brief
glimpse of what's coming for us. What we face here is nothing

compared to the glory we'll see on the other side. It's all just part of the journey.

> "To endure the cross is not tragedy; it is the suffering which is the fruit of an exclusive allegiance to Jesus Christ."
>
> -Dietrich Bonhoeffer

Work out your salvation

Philippians 2:12-13 Therefore, my beloved, as you have always obeyed, so now, not only as in my presence but much more in my absence, work out your own salvation with fear and trembling, for it is God who works in you, both to will and to work for his good pleasure.

Though we can't earn salvation through good works, not all of the effects of salvation can be seen immediately in us and we're called to persevere in our faith and "work out" our salvation. As we progress in our walk with Christ, God works in and through us.

At the point we would call conversion, we do become new creations[1], our old nature dying and our new nature being in Christ. It's through persevering faith, though, that we really take on the new attributes of a Christ-follower, the fruits. The Holy Spirit works in us "to will and to work for His good pleasure". This means our very desires begin to change because of God's work in us. We don't just change because we think we're supposed to change, we change because we now desire to do so. Our wants begin to align with God's will and purpose.

---

1   (2 Corinthians 5:17)

When we follow Christ, we take on His plans as our own and God has us bring about His will by transforming us to be more like Him.

One excuse people give for not turning their lives over to Christ is that they need to clean up their act first. Make no mistake, it works the other way around. You come to Christ and HE cleans up your life.

Number our days

Psalm 90:12 So teach us to number our days that we may get a heart
of wisdom.

This life on earth is like a breath. Before we can know what happened, it's come to an end. No matter how much effort we put into gaining things for ourselves – possessions, wealth, prestige, pleasure – we leave everything behind in the end. As the saying goes, "You can't take it with you."

As followers of Christ, we should be seeking to prioritize our time in this short existence to use our time in the way God wants us to. Our prayer should mimic the Psalm, asking God to teach us to number our days, that we may know Him more fully and bring about His will. Our desire should be for a heart of wisdom.

Two practical applications for learning to number your days: seek the guidance of the Holy Spirit and store up God's Word in your heart[1]. Make the most of what God's given you.

---

1   (Psalm 119:11)

Living Stones

1 Peter 2:5 you yourselves like living stones are being built up as a spiritual house, to be a holy priesthood, to offer spiritual sacrifices acceptable to God through Jesus Christ.

Where does God dwell? Is He confined to the walls of a church? Limited to operating on Sunday mornings? Or is God's house a spiritual one, made of living stones?

In the Old Testament, the Lord had the people of Israel construct a temple, that He might dwell among them there[2]. For generations, the tradition was that the temple was God's dwelling place. Jesus came and turned everything upside down. On several occasions, Jesus made reference to destroying the temple and rebuilding it. He did this to illustrate how He would be killed and rise from the dead.

He, the stone that the builders (religious leaders) rejected, became the cornerstone (foundation) to the Church. Now we are the living stones that make up the Church, it's no longer about a building, but a people. The church is alive and continuously growing and being built up. Each Christian is part of the priesthood and through their lives offering up

---

2   (see Exodus)

spiritual sacrifices. We have direct access to God.

We are the Church, the body of Christ. We will bring about His kingdom, regardless of building or location.

To be clear: meeting together in a church setting is still very important and I don't want to make it sound like I'm taking away from this. The point, however, is that the Church is made up of the believers, not the bricks. We're each God's temple, because He lives in us.

A choice to make

1 John 2:15 Do not love the world or the things in the world. If anyone loves the world, the love of the Father is not in him. For all that is in the world—the desires of the flesh and the desires of the eyes and pride in possessions—is not from the Father but is from the world. And the world is passing away along with its desires, but whoever does the will of God abides forever.

You know from Jesus' own words that you can't serve two masters[1]. If you're fully devoted to God, you can't be devoted to this world. There are good things in the world, after all, God created it. But He created it for His glory and when we devote ourselves to the creation instead of the Creator, we find ourselves in sin.

There are a lot of tempting things all around us. Things that, if we allow ourselves to be distracted, can consume us. Possessions can possess us and desires can overtake us. There's only one way to overcome the world and it's to follow the One who overcomes the world[2]. The One who created and sustains it can use us while we're here on this earth, but only if we choose Him over all of this.

---

1   (Matthew 6:24)
2   (John 16:33)

There are no regrets to be had if we pass up sin. The things here that seem so wonderful are fleeting, they're dying. But when they're all gone, the Lord will endure through all eternity. His love never fails.

Some people are afraid to turn their lives over to Christ because they're afraid of what they'll have to give up. The reality is that your desires begin to match His as you grow closer to Him and you don't feel like you're giving anything up at all.

Worshipping false idols

*Habakkuk 2:18 What profit is an idol when its maker has shaped it,
a metal image, a teacher of lies? For its maker trusts in his own
creation when he makes speechless idols!*

As we look through the Old Testament of the Bible and see
many examples of idol worship, it's easy to arrogantly think that
we've come so far from that way of life. It seems so silly that
someone would fashion an idol out of wood or bronze and
then worship something that they had just created. We know
in our minds that God is the one worthy of worship as the
Creator, but still we do worship the created.

Don't think that this is true today? How about extreme
environmentalism where man worships the earth, which God
created? Or how about trusting in money to get you everything
you want from position to health to security? Some of us even
worship our own children, building our entire lives around
their little needs and wants. We do worship idols that aren't
worthy of our full devotion. There's nothing wrong with taking
care of the earth, earning money, or loving your children. All of
those are good things. But when they are the main focus of our
lives, they are our gods.

Habakkuk rightly points out the absurdity of putting our trust in and directing our worship towards idols we've created and expecting them to better our lives somehow. Only God Himself is worthy to be praised and He deserves our full attention and devotion.

> "Oh! if your heart swims in the rays of God's love, like a little mote swimming in the sunbeam, you will have no room in your heart for idols."
>
> -Robert Murray McCheyne

Say no to sin

Proverbs 1:10 My son, if sinners entice you, do not consent.

Who are your friends? Whose approval do you seek out? If your friends don't encourage you to do the will of God, don't listen to them. It can be quite a struggle to do the right thing sometimes because we all want to be liked, but likeability is not listed as a biblical virtue. Sometimes, as the saying goes, the right thing is not the popular thing.

All around us, we're being enticed into sin. The TV ads try to sell us on it, the popular culture flaunts it, and sadly some churches even embrace it or excuse it. But there's only one voice that we should be following, and it's the one of Him who created us. God knows what's best, even if we think sin will be fun for a while. He cares for us and has a plan for each one of us.

The truth is that sin only appears pleasing and in the end it leads to death and decay. Following the Lord is where we find true joy and true fulfillment.

Confess your sins

1 John 1:8-9 If we say we have no sin, we deceive ourselves, and the truth is not in us. If we confess our sins, he is faithful and just to forgive us our sins and to cleanse us from all unrighteousness.

With many things in this life, we can expect to get out of them exactly what we put into them. If we treat people rudely, we'll often find ourselves being treated rudely. If we disrespect, we'll be disrespected. Acting out of pride usually leads to resistance, and humility leads to better things. This is especially true with God[1].

When we pretend that we don't sin, no one is fooled. We can't even truly fool ourselves into thinking we're sinless let alone God. But when we put our pride aside and admit to our wrongs, God is quick to forgive because of Christ Jesus. There's nothing to fear in confession before God. He's a loving and just Father who actually wants to forgive us. He's waiting for us to turn to Him.

The bad news is that you have sinned and there's no way out of it. The good news is Jesus paid your way to God's forgiveness by taking all of your sins onto Himself. You're free to confess

---

1   (James 4:6)

everything, with no fear of condemnation. Our Lord is able
and willing to wipe it all away.

> *"The confession of evil works is the first beginning of good works."*
>
> *- Augustine*

There's a way out

1 Corinthians 10:13 No temptation has overtaken you that is not common to man. God is faithful, and he will not let you be tempted beyond your ability, but with the temptation he will also provide the way of escape, that you may be able to endure it.

So you know by now that sin is bad and that you should choose to stay away from it. But it isn't always just that simple, is it? Sometimes the temptation to sin is great and just knowing that it's wrong isn't enough. It can be overwhelming.

But there's good news! God is looking out for you. If you belong to Him, He's on your side and He provides a way fro you to stay true to Him. The Holy Spirit working in you will not only nudge you to let you know when something is sin, He'll point you to a way of escape from the temptation.

No matter how massive the temptation you're facing, God has seen it before, Jesus has faced it before[1], and the Spirit has dealt with it before. You're not alone and you don't have to face any sin or any temptation without help. The truth is, you have the greatest help ever available because God Himself is cheering for you to win. Find assurance in that.

---

1   (Hebrews 4:15)

When everything falls apart

Colossians 1:16-17 For by him all things were created, in heaven and on earth, visible and invisible, whether thrones or dominions or rulers or authorities—all things were created through him and for him. And he is before all things, and in him all things hold together.

These times we're living in are difficult, to say the least. With economic meltdown and employment instability, it's no wonder why so many people are filled with anxiety. Add to that moral decay that brings about all kinds of evil deeds and the times can be downright frightening.

But as Christians, those who belong to God, we have hope beyond the hope that this world has to offer. The very same God who created everything holds it all together. This very Jesus by whom and for whom all things were created sustains all of it. No matter what your situation, He is not ignorant of what's going on. No matter how bad it seems, all things are in His hands.

Give over your troubles to Him and He will take care of you[1]. There's no problem in your life too big for our Lord.

---

1 (Matthew 11:28-30)

When times are good

Deuteronomy 8:11 Take care lest you forget the Lord your God by not keeping his commandments and his rules and his statutes, which I command you today

One lesson we could all stand to learn is that God not only sustains us through the hard times, but the good times are from Him as well. It's easy to find ourselves crying out to God in the midst of our struggles only to forget about Him when He brings us through them and things get better. Do you know it's because of Him that things improved?

Moses knew this. The Israelites wandered for forty years in the wilderness before they got to inhabit the land God had promised them. They had seen many hardships along the way, and Moses was always reminding them to rely on God. When the time came to claim their inheritance, Moses strongly warned them not to forget God in all their prosperity[2]. We can sometimes become so focused on the gifts that we disregard the Giver.

Make no mistake, our Lord is the Giver of all. No blessing in

---

2   (Deuteronomy 8:1-20)

your life could exist apart from Him and His mercy and grace. Don't forget about Him when the times are good.

> *"We can stand affliction better than we can prosperity, for in prosperity we forget God."*
>
> *- D.L. Moody*

The Law

Colossians 2:20-23 If with Christ you died to the elemental spirits of the world, why, as if you were still alive in the world, do you submit to regulations— "Do not handle, Do not taste, Do not touch" (referring to things that all perish as they are used)—according to human precepts and teachings? These have indeed an appearance of wisdom in promoting self-made religion and asceticism and severity to the body, but they are of no value in stopping the indulgence of the flesh.

What is Christianity all about? Have we vowed to follow Christ only to replace the Old Testament law with new law? Is this new life just about more rule-following? Observing some of today's churches, you would think so! Sermons so often focus on behavior modification or bettering the life of the Christian through specific actions. Congregants lack the joy of Christ because they fail to keep up with all of the things they are "supposed" to do.

The truth is that no formula for behavior modification will ever work because the root of sin is in our hearts. No amount of keeping up with strict law or disciplines or rituals will keep us from being what we are: fallen and sinful. Religion seeks to justify the believer through their actions. True justification comes from Christ[1]. Only He can liberate us from sin.

It can make us feel good for a while to try to earn our own merit, but in the end we will always fall short[2]. We'll never be good enough, do enough, deprive ourselves enough to be free from sin. If we fully rely on Jesus it means we trust that His sacrifice was good enough, that we don't need to be under the law in order to receive forgiveness from God for our transgressions, that He died once, and for all[3].

1   (Romans 4:25)
2   (Romans 3:23)
3   (Hebrews 7:27-28)

God helps those...

John 15:5 I am the vine; you are the branches. If a man remains in me and I in him, he will bear much fruit; apart from me you can do nothing.

One of the most often quoted theological statements is "God helps those who help themselves". The troubling thing about basing one's view of God on this idea is that it's just not biblical (The statement itself is most often attributed to Benjamin Franklin). One of the main themes of the Bible is that man is incapable of helping himself. Apart from God we are depraved, unable to life ourselves out of the pit that sin has led us to. We cannot help ourselves.

But God, in His sovereignty, chooses to help us anyway. While we were still sinners, Christ died for us[1]. In other words, He helped us though we were not helping ourselves. Even if we tried to gain some ground without God, our best efforts are useless[2]. Our Lord knew we would be helpless. His plan is to be our refuge, our shelter[3], our comforter[4], our advocate[5]. The

---

1   (Romans 5:8)
2   (Isaiah 64:6)
3   (Isaiah 25:4)
4   (John 14:16)
5   (1 John 2:1)

list goes on. Why would God have such descriptive names of one who defends and provides for the helpless if we were able to doing anything for ourselves?

Secular theology may find it reasonable to accept that we must do something to earn God's favor, but to the Christian it's irreconcilable with The Word. God helps those who cannot help themselves.

> "What is meant by the concept of total depravity is not that man is wicked as he could possibly be. Bad as we are, we can still conceive of ourselves doing worse things than we do. Rather, it means that sin has such a hold upon us in our natural state, that we never have a positive desire for Christ."
>
> -R.C. Sproul

The power of prayer

Psalm 66:20 Praise be to God, who has not rejected my prayer or withheld his love from me!

We've often heard testimonies given of miracles that have taken place in the lives of those who tell them. On many of those occasions, the recipient of the miracle gives credit to "the power of prayer". The question is: Is this putting us in the place of God? Are we, if only in a veiled way, taking the credit for the miracle because we prayed for it?

Just to be clear, prayer is in fact quite powerful for those who believe[1]. There are many instances throughout the Bible in which we are called to pray, with faith. The issue is not the effectiveness of praying, rather it's about who gets the credit after the prayer has been answered.

We must recognize that when a prayer is answered it is because God chose to respond with favor. The sovereign Lord is the one who decides what is right for us. It's not the act of prayer itself that has granted us what we desire. It's not we who have manifested this miracle. The real power is God's.

---

1 (James 5:16)

Believe and it's yours?

Mark 11:24 Therefore I tell you, whatever you ask for in prayer, believe that you have received it, and it will be yours.

The fact is that prayer is so powerful that it has been exploited and misused by those who have no intentions of serving God. Those who seek after their own selfish desires on this earth have used the very gift God gave us to connect with Him and perverted it, made it into some genie-in-a-bottle formula for getting things. God did not intend prayer to be a vending machine.

Yes, Jesus clearly said that whatever we ask for in His name shall be ours, but we must remember that He said this to His disciples. Jesus made this statement with the understanding that those who heard it had left everything behind to follow Him. They had given up more comfortable lives to serve the Son of God. That doesn't mean the promise isn't ours to claim as well, it simply means that there are stipulations attached.

Those who follow Christ and call themselves disciples seek to bring Him honor and glory and in doing so pray for His will. If we are seeking Christ, the desires of our heart will not be selfish and our prayers will reflect the character of God. If we're walking with the Lord, our desires will be in line with His desires.

> "Real prayer is communion with God, so that there will be common thoughts between His mind and ours. What is needed is for Him to fill our hearts with His thoughts, and then His desires will become our desires flowing back to Him."
>
> *-A. W. Pink*

The voice of a man

Joshua 10:12-14 At that time Joshua spoke to the Lord in the day when the Lord gave the Amorites over to the sons of Israel, and he said in the sight of Israel, "Sun, stand still at Gibeon, and moon, in the Valley of Aijalon." And the sun stood still, and the moon stopped, until the nation took vengeance on their enemies. Is this not written in the Book of Jashar? The sun stopped in the midst of heaven and did not hurry to set for about a whole day. There has been no day like it before or since, when the Lord heeded the voice of a man, for the Lord fought for Israel.

What would you pray for if you knew God would hear you and answer? What would you have the faith to believe Him for if you knew, with no doubt or fear, that He was on your side?

The story of Joshua praying for the sun to stand still in the sky is often centered around his bold prayer and God's answer, but shift your focus just for a moment back on verse 8 of this story. Notice that before Joshua had the bold faith to pray for a mighty miracle, he heard from God. The Lord told Joshua that He was on his side and that Israel would win over their enemies.

With that knowledge, Joshua was able to pray with complete

faith, knowing that God was with him. We too can be courageous in our prayers if we first hear from God that He is on our side. Are you living for Him? Is He on your side? Consult God's Word and find where He wants you. When you are there, He is fighting on your side, and your voice too will be heard.

> "If the size of your vision for your life isn't intimidating to you, there's a good chance it's insulting to God."
>
> *-Steven Furtick*

He hears us

1 John 5:14-15 And this is the confidence that we have toward him, that if we ask anything according to his will he hears us. And if we know that he hears us in whatever we ask, we know that we have the requests that we have asked of him.

Joshua prayed with confidence because he knew that God would hear his prayers. God had told him earlier that He was on Joshua's side. The apostle John also knew the value of approaching God in prayer with confidence.

If we know that He hears us, we know He'll grant us all that we ask accordingly with His will. To pray according to His will though, we must be daily in His Word, seeking Him. When we're in close communion with our heavenly Father, we'll know what we can ask for and expect to be heard. With that, we can ask with confidence.

Knowing that our Father loves us and cares for us makes a world of difference as we approach Him. Thankful hearts, knowing that He hears us, make it all the more likely that we'll ask according to His will.

Ask, seek, knock

Luke 11:9-10 And I tell you, ask, and it will be given to you; seek, and you will find; knock, and it will be opened to you. For everyone who asks receives, and the one who seeks finds, and to the one who knocks it will be opened.

After Jesus had taught His disciples how they should pray[1], and that they should pray with perseverance[2], He tells them that if they ask of God they will receive.

If our earthly fathers know how to give us good things, how much more does our heavenly Father know exactly what we need and how to give it to us? We never have to worry when we pray because the Lord is good and He is capable of providing anything and everything.

Luke's account of this story does not say that God will give "good things" like Matthew's[3], but rather that the Father will give the Holy Spirit to those who ask Him. What better gift could we ever receive from God but the gift of Himself? He is more than we could ever imagine or think to ask for.

---

1   (v.2-4)
2   (v.5-8)
3   (Matthew 7:7-11)

The Lord loves to bless His people. He wants us to ask for all that He has in store for us. In the end, it brings Him glory.

> "When we ask of the Lord cooly, and not fervently, we do as it were, stop His hand, and restrain Him from giving us the very blessing we "pretend" that we are seeking."
>
> -Charles Spurgeon

Love never fails

1 Corinthians 13:8 Love never ends.

There's one thing in this world that will never end, can never be defeated by the forces of darkness and continues on into the next life. God's love never ends, it never fails, and there's nothing we can do to affect His love for us. The Lord is sovereign and He will chose whom to love.

It should be noted that nowhere in all of Paul's descriptions of what love is and is not does he ever refer to it as an emotion. Love is so far beyond just being something we feel, though we make it out to be nothing more. We talk of "falling in love" and then "falling out of love", but that just isn't characteristic of love at all. Love cannot be fallen into or fallen out of because it's an action, not a whim. Loving is a choice, and we must choose to love everyday.

God's love for us is unconditional, not based on feelings or circumstances. He chooses to love us, just as we should choose to love those around us, regardless of whether or not they deserve it. Love never fails, it can never be defeated, and it will endure forever. When God chose to sacrifice His Son on the cross to take on the punishment we deserved for our sins, love won, once and for all.

"Genuine love is not merely a feeling or an involuntary attraction. It involves a willful choice, and that is why (the word is often) in the form of an imperative. Far from being something we "fall into" by happenstance, authentic love involves a deliberate, voluntary commitment to sacrifice whatever we can for the good of the person we love."

-John MacArthur

The Rock

1 Corinthians 10:4 and all drank the same spiritual drink. For they drank from the spiritual Rock that followed them, and the Rock was Christ.

Every bit of the Bible, from Genesis to Revelation, points us to Jesus. The foreshadowing given, the pictures painted, all are for the glory of God and to teach us about His character. The Old Testament and the Law set up the coming Christ and His fulfillment of the Law. Study of God's Word can teach us lessons we never realized could be learned from these stories.

Paul shows us, in His letter to the church in Corinth, that the story of Moses in the wilderness with the children of Israel is more than just a story. The rock that Moses struck[1] was more than just a rock, and this was more than just God showing His power. This, like so many other biblical illustrations, points us to Jesus, who is The Rock. In Him we find living water, water better than that which flowed to the thirsty people of Israel.

But this is also an illustration of what happens when we corrupt what is of God and celebrate it as man's own[2]. The

---

1   (Exodus 17:6)
2   (Numbers 20:10-11)

story of Moses striking the rock when God told him only to speak to it is a look at how we can be so quick to disobey God and make an idol out of our own achievements. Moses knew that once he had make water come from a rock by striking it with his stick, so when God told him to speak to the rock, Moses disobeyed and tried to repeat his previous feat. Moses took what was good and corrupted it. You know the rest of the story, he didn't get to enter into the promised land with his people. Even with a great man like Moses, God didn't tolerate idolatry.

Jesus is the true Rock, He is the source of all things good. Because we've experienced His goodness in the past, we can be too quick to assume that we had something to do with the blessings and try to get the same results in our own strength. This is idolatry, making ourselves into our own gods. There is only one Rock that has the water of life, and it's Jesus.

Give everything

Passage: Mark 14:3-9

Key verse: Mark 14:3 And while he was at Bethany in the house of Simon the leper, as he was reclining at table, a woman came with an alabaster flask of ointment of pure nard, very costly, and she broke the flask and poured it over his head

In the days leading up to Jesus' death on the cross, He taught some of the greatest lessons of His earthly ministry. At Bethany, days before His crucifixion, Jesus was anointed for burial by a woman willing to give all she had. Here we can all learn about sacrifice.

While some plotted to kill Jesus, His disciples remained in denial about His certain death, despite many warnings. The woman at Bethany, however, stood apart from everyone else. Her concern was not with who would be the greatest, or how much money she could get for selling her oil. Her mind was set on full devotion to Jesus. Sitting at the feet of the Lord, she anointed Him with the costly oil. It's a picture of how much more He meant to her than her earthly possessions did.

Are you willing to give it all in full devotion to Jesus Christ?

Can you say that you've given your whole life to Him? Is following Him more important than anything else? Jesus gave Himself, suffering on a cross, willing to be considered cursed, for the sake of our reconciliation with God. Heaven was bankrupted of its most precious treasure all for us. Now what are we willing to give up?

The new covenant

Passage: Matthew 26:26-29

Key verse: Matthew 26:28 for this is my blood of the covenant, which is poured out for many for the forgiveness of sins.

Long before Jesus' earthly ministry, God made a covenant with His people[1]. In Christ, that covenant was fulfilled and a new covenant was made. No longer would the Lord's people be forced to make sacrifices upon an altar. Once and for all, the ultimate sacrifice was paid. Jesus was sent to be the only sacrifice that could ever truly cleanse us of our sin. He is the spotless lamb[2].

Before being led off to die a horrifying death, Jesus ate one last meal with His closest followers. Here He gave them a picture of what was to happen, whether they understood it or not. His instructions to them were to remember Him through the practice of taking communion, the Lord's Supper. The bread is symbolic of His broken body that was sacrificially given for our sake. The wine, His blood, that poured out as He was tortured in our place.

---

1   (Exodus 24:8)
2   (1 Peter 1:18-19)

Reflect on what Christ gave so that you and I can live free and in communion with God. We have life because He gave His, let's remember all that entails regularly and practice that remembrance with others.

Betrayed beyond belief

Passage: John 13:1-20

Key verse: Matthew 26:21 And as they were eating, he said, "Truly, I say to you, one of you will betray me."

No one, in the history of mankind, ever experienced the level of betrayal that the Son of God did. Would you agree? Nothing you've ever faced comes close to His time on earth. Yet look at how Jesus dealt with those who betrayed Him, denied Him, abandoned Him, falsely accused Him, beat Him, tortured Him, and killed Him.

In light of the fact that Jesus knew all things before they occurred, John 13:1 is particularly powerful. Knowing full well how His own disciples would treat Him, He "loved them to the end". Wow. Park there for a minute.

With all knowledge that Peter would deny Him, that Judas would betray Him, and that the rest would run away, Jesus knelt down before each of them, taking on the role of a servant, and washed the feet of each man.

What right on this earth do you and I have to be unforgiving toward anyone who's wronged us? We have to be amazed at this action and attitude by Jesus because He of all people did have the right to judge and withhold forgiveness. Can we follow His example?

Denied

Key verses: Luke 22:61-62 And the Lord turned and looked at Peter. And Peter remembered the saying of the Lord, how he had said to him, "Before the rooster crows today, you will deny me three times." And he went out and wept bitterly.

After all Jesus had done for Peter, how could he deny his Lord? That's the question we all ask, isn't it? How could this man who walked so closely with the Son of God deny even knowing Him? But the truth is, Jesus did more for you and me than He did for Peter and even we deny Him. The real question is: How could WE?

At the time of Peter's denial, Jesus had yet to suffer on a cross, taking on the sins of the world, dying that we might have reconciliation with God. But in our time, He has already paid that price, finished that purpose. We have all the more reason to give Him the praise due Him, but instead we sometimes choose our own way and leave Him out of the equation.

The good news for Peter is that Christ still died for him, despite his denial. Later, He even gave Peter a chance to

121

redeem himself[1]. The good news for us is that He did die for our sake and we're still able to call on Him. Just like for Peter, our denial is not the end of the story. Right now, at this moment, we can follow Him.

---

1   (John 21:15-19)

The high priestly prayer

Passage: John 17:1-26

Key verse: John 17:1:24 Father, I desire that they also, whom you have given me, may be with me where I am, to see my glory that you have given me because you loved me before the foundation of the world.

Before the world was created, Jesus was. Before time began, Jesus was. And then, the Eternal One who holds all things in balance did something extraordinary – He stepped into time and took on human flesh. He gave up all the glory of heaven so that we could know God. He gave up many of His rights as God, but one thing He did not give up – His love for us.

While on this earth, Jesus loved His own just as He loved them in heaven. In His last hours, He prayed a beautiful prayer, first for His close followers and then for you and me. He knew He was betrayed, He knew He would die, and He knew that you and I would sin against Him. But He prayed a high priestly prayer for our joy in Him, our unity in Him, our sanctification in Him.

Then Jesus gave us an idea of what salvation is all about. He died that we might be where He is, that we may see His glory and therefore glorify the Father. This was the plan before time began. He's always loved us, before we even existed. And though we've sinned against Him, He chose to die in our place, taking our sins onto Himself, so that we can experience eternal life with Him. What love He has for us.

The atonement

Passage: Luke 23:26-49

Key verses: Galatians 3:13 Christ redeemed us from the curse of the law by becoming a curse for us—for it is written, "Cursed is everyone who is hanged on a tree"[1]

Entire courses are taught at universities just to try and explain Jesus' work on the cross. The atonement is not easy to understand, but it is simple. God came down to earth in human flesh, lived a sinless life, and then died as the one true spotless sacrifice that could take away our sins. Without this one truth, all the rest falls apart.

Jesus took on our sins. Jesus, the perfect Son of God, took on our sins upon Himself. He took our punishment, bought our redemption. That is the only reason you and I will ever see heaven. It's not because of how many good deeds we did or how nice we are. It's because we were bought and paid for by the blood of Christ. Let that sink in. Weep over the fact that it was necessary.

My sins nailed Him to that cross. Your sins drove those spikes

---

1   See also 2 Corinthians 5:21

125

in. Our rejection of God killed Him. And He chose to be there. As the one, true, all-powerful God, He could have ended this any way He wanted. But He chose the cross. He chose suffering in our place. Because He loved us, even before we existed. That's the truth of the cross.

Forgiveness in Christ

Passage: John 19:28-30

Key verses: Colossians 1:13-14 He has delivered us from the domain of darkness and transferred us to the kingdom of his beloved Son, in whom we have redemption, the forgiveness of sins.

Since the sin of our first parents, we've been on the path of destruction. Only perfection can enter into the kingdom of heaven and we're tainted. Our sinful nature bought for us a ticket straight to eternity away from God. But the story doesn't end there.

You see, God couldn't let it end that way. He loved His creation far too much to let us have what we deserved, so in the ultimate act of love, Jesus became flesh, God bankrupted heaven of its treasure, and He delivered us from destruction. Our debt was paid in His sacrifice. Everything we owed was paid in full when He died on that cross. He transferred us to His kingdom, a life spent with God, not apart from Him. He redeemed us.

In Christ we have full forgiveness. Our slate is clean, our record is wiped out. We owe Him everything, because He has set us free. In Him we have life. His death finished the work

that He was sent here to do. But still the story doesn't end
there. No, that part of the story gets us to Friday – but Sunday
is the part that makes it all mean something. Sunday is the
main event.

> *"God blesses his people with extravagant grace so they might*
> *extend his extravagant glory to all peoples on the earth."*
>
> *-David Platt*

He is risen!

Passage: Matthew 28:1-10

Key verses: Matthew 28:6 He is not here, for he has risen, as he said.
Come, see the place where he lay.
1 Corinthians 15:14 And if Christ has not been raised, then our
preaching is in vain and your faith is in vain.

The truth about the work of Christ on the cross, the
forgiveness of our sins, and our reconciliation with God is that
it all means nothing if our God is still lying in a tomb. Jesus
can't mediate between God and man if He's dead. If His death
is the end, then we're no better off.

But – our God lives. He isn't dead. Death couldn't hold Him.
Hell couldn't defeat Him. He is risen. He lives. And because
He lives, we live. Jesus' departure back into heaven is hope for
us all that we'll be resurrected as well, taken from this life into
the next, never to die again. But it means something now too.

Because Jesus departed, God sent the Holy Spirit to live within
us. His departure means we now act on His behalf as
Christians, and He's empowered us to do so. No other religion
on earth can make these claims because no other religion has a
living Savior. We have a God so loving that He would sacrifice

His Son in our place, and that God is so powerful that death cannot be the end for Him. HE IS RISEN!

> *"The validity of our faith and the legitimacy of our hope are dependent on the reality of the resurrection of Jesus."*
>
> *-Mark Driscoll*

Jesus, the Son

Galatians 4:4-7 But when the fullness of time had come, God sent forth his Son, born of woman, born under the law, to redeem those who were under the law, so that we might receive adoption as sons. And because you are sons, God has sent the Spirit of his Son into our hearts, crying, "Abba! Father!" So you are no longer a slave, but a son, and if a son, then an heir through God.

God exists eternally in the form of three equal, but distinct persons: The Father, the Son, the Holy Spirit. Often when we talk about "God" we're referring to God the Father. But how can God, who is spirit, and exists outside of time, be a father? And how can three be one? The answer to these types of questions are not easy to explain, but the Bible does help us understand.

All three persons of the Trinity have existed since before time[1]. No one gave birth to the Son, He's always existed. Not until He came to dwell on the earth as a man was He birthed of a woman, and even then by choice. Jesus, the Father, and the Spirit are all equal, of the same substance[2]. His place as Son is not lesser than the Father, so verses like John 14:28 speak to

---

1   (John 1)
2   (John 10:30)

purpose and not to rank. Jesus' purpose is to glorify the Father, just as the Spirit is to bring glory to Jesus.

Further, His place as Son gives us a picture of just how God wants us to be. God sent His only Son with the purpose that we also might become His sons, and if sons then heirs to everything Christ is entitled to. This word sons isn't gender related and doesn't exclude women, it does the opposite. There's power in using the word sons because traditionally sons have received a greater inheritance. By including females as His "sons", God has granted all the same rights to His riches. By accepting Christ, we became sons of God. And Jesus is the "firstborn" among us.

Jesus, the Creator

John 1:3 All things were made through him, and without him was not any thing made that was made.

Jesus, the Savior of the world, the One who was sent to redeem mankind, is the Creator of mankind. How so? If there is only one God and He exists as three persons[1] and He has existed from eternity...then how is Jesus not the Creator?

The apostle John comes right out of the gates with his theology. No lineages, no birth story in a manger in Bethlehem – right to the point – Jesus is God. "In the beginning was the Word[2], and the Word was with God and the Word was God." Wait, it gets even more clear: "All things were made through him, and without him was not any thing made that was made." Don't believe John? How about Paul? "For by Him[3], all things were created, in heaven and on earth, visible and invisible..."[4].

How does it change your view of God to think about how the God who created us is the very same God who came to save us? Our Creator is our Redeemer. The One who holds all things

---

1   (Father, Son, Holy Spirit)
2   (Jesus, the logos)
3   (Jesus)
4   (Colossians 1:15)

together is the One who gave His life that we might be with Him. How's that for love? Does it change how you see Jesus? He's not just some baby we celebrate on Christmas or just some guy with a beard who taught good moral lessons. It all began with Him. And it all ends with Him.

Jesus, the King

Ephesians 1:20-21 that he worked in Christ when he raised him from the dead and seated him at his right hand in the heavenly places, far above all rule and authority and power and dominion, and above every name that is named, not only in this age but also in the one to come.

Long ago, God's people asked Him for a king to rule over them[1]. Though they were warned against such a thing, they still demanded to be ruled by a king. God granted their request, but the history of Israel is full of men who let them down, kings who couldn't live up to the expectations placed on them. Many of these men did not even follow God. But that was under the old covenant.

Today, God's people live under the new covenant of Christ. Jesus was appointed our King and His reign will never end. He will never disappoint because He is fully God. He will never lead us astray because He knows all things and He is good. He will never fail because all things have been placed under His dominion. His kingdom will know no end. At the very name of Jesus, every knee will bow, in heaven and on earth and under the earth, and every tongue will confess that He is Lord, to the

---

1   (I Samuel 8)

glory of God the Father[2].

He came to this earth, not to establish an earthly kingdom
(though He could have), but to grant access to His heavenly
kingdom – where nothing can destroy what He has created. To
what king do you pledge your allegiance?

---

*"'Safe?' said Mr. Beaver. 'Who said anything about safe? 'Course he
isn't safe, but he's good. He's the King, I tell you.'"*
                    - C.S. Lewis, The Lion, the Witch and the Wardrobe

---

Jesus, the Messiah

John 4:25-26 The woman said to him, "I know that Messiah is coming (he who is called Christ). When he comes, he will tell us all things." Jesus said to her, "I who speak to you am he."

For many years, God's people waited for a promised Messiah, the Chosen One who God would send to save them and redeem them. They waited eagerly, expectantly. But when the Messiah arrived, when He was right in front of them – they didn't recognize Him.

For the Jews, the Messiah was going to be a powerful conqueror who would crash the scene and free them from their oppressors. Then he would establish his kingdom and they'd all live happily ever after. But things didn't happen that way. Jesus didn't come riding on a stallion, shooting fireballs at the Romans. No, He first came as a baby born in a stable, then He was a carpenter, then a traveling rabbi with no place to call home – a servant to those around Him.

He didn't come to be served, but to serve[1]. No wonder they couldn't recognize Him as the Messiah! But He did come to free His people – not only them but also any who would follow

---

1   (Mark 10:45)

after Him, Jews or otherwise. He didn't just free them from their earthly oppressors but from spiritual strongholds, from sin, from condemnation.

Whether they saw it or not, Jesus was the Messiah God had promised long ago. He conquered sin and death and His kingdom knows no end.

Jesus, the sacrificial lamb

*John 1:29 The next day he saw Jesus coming toward him, and said,
"Behold, the Lamb of God, who takes away the sin of the world!*

The entire Bible is the story of Jesus. Long before He came to
earth as a baby in a manger, God showed His people pictures of
the future. When Abraham was set to sacrifice Isaac, a
scapegoat was provided in his place[1]. When the Israelites in
Egypt were preparing to flee with Moses, God had them shed
the blood of a spotless lamb so that death would pass over
them. Then, the perfect Lamb of God entered the scene.

All along, God had been telling the story of Jesus through the
lives of His people. Then He sent His own sacrificial Lamb.
But this sacrifice was good enough to cover all sins – once, and
for all. Only Jesus, who lived among His creation, facing the
same temptations as you and I, but without sinning, could take
all of the sins of the world onto Himself. Only He could
provide that sacrifice for redemption. Only He could bring
justification.

John the Baptist saw it right away when he declared Jesus "the
Lamb of God who takes away the sins of the world". Paul

---

1   (Genesis 22:1-19)

understood the symbolism when he spoke of Jesus as "our passover lamb"[1]. Do you see Him for what He is? He bought your freedom with His life.

> Only Jesus could be both the Lion and the Lamb, the all-powerful ruler over all things and the loving Savior who gave His own life voluntarily for the lives of His people.

---

1 (1 Corinthians 5:7)

Jesus, the risen Lord

Luke 24:5b-6a "Why do you seek the living among the dead? He is not here, but has risen.

Why do we look for the living among the dead? Just as those who lived with Jesus while He was on the earth, we can tend to look for Jesus in the tomb. But He's not there. Some think of Jesus with some sentimentality, as though He was once great, but now lives powerless in the grave. But He's not there. He is alive.

If Jesus was not resurrected, He would be unable to act as our intercessor today. But because He lives, He mediates between God and man. Because He lives, He has the power to act as Lord. Our God is not a dead god. Our God has all power and authority.

What other god ever loved his own people so much that he would sacrifice his own life to save them? Who, in the history of mankind, ever sacrificed himself only to rise from the dead? Only one. Jesus Christ, the Son of God, gave His own life for us but lives now to act on our behalf. He lives so we live. If this wasn't true, our faith would be in one who was powerless to be Lord of all. But He does live. And He is Lord of all.

Jesus, the healer

Acts 3:6 But Peter said, "I have no silver and gold, but what I do have I give to you. In the name of Jesus Christ of Nazareth, rise up and walk!"

Many accounts are given in the New Testament of Jesus healing people. From the blind, to the lame, to the dead, Jesus is the ultimate physician. When He heals, God Himself has made someone well. Of course it's fascinating to watch events unfold as the Son of God lays hands on the sick and brings them to health. But it's also noteworthy that the very power of His name caused some to be healed.

Those who had walked the earth with Jesus knew His power. Peter, who had walked on water and seen his Lord calm the storms, knew what Christ was capable of. He had confidence that it was not he who would heal the sick, but Christ's power through Him. He claimed that power and gave it and he used it in ministry.

The power of Christ in us can do more than heal physical ailments. He can heal broken hearts, mend broken relationships, reconcile sinners to God, and regenerate hearts and lives. If there's anything that can be broken, He can fix it.

If there's anything that can deteriorate, He can heal it. There's nothing outside His ability as the great Healer.

> "The miracles Jesus performs... do not compel faith; but those with faith will perceive their significance."
>
> -D.A. Carson

Jesus, the provider

Philippians 4:19 And my God will supply every need of yours according to his riches in glory in Christ Jesus.

There is only one who is capable of providing for your every need. No matter what you lack, He's got it in stock. You see, everything is His. He owns all things. As the Psalmist put it, the "cattle on a thousand hills" are His[1]. Since He owns everything, He's capable of providing anything you could ever need. He lacks nothing.

"This is God!" you say, and yes it is. God the Father does provide our every need but notice that He gives "according to His riches in glory in Christ Jesus." God's riches, all of His treasure, is in the glory of Jesus! When Jesus was sent to this earth to die for our sins, heaven was literally bankrupted of all its riches. God put it all on the line, every chip was on the table.

Jesus is our Great Provider. Just as He supplied endless food from just a small amount of bread and fish, He can give us all we need. Do we trust in Him to do just that?

---

1   (Psalm 50:10)

Jesus, the teacher

John 13:15 For I have given you an example, that you also should do just as I have done to you.

Many people, even non-Christians, would say that Jesus was a good teacher. From the sermon on the mount to His parables, people love Jesus the teacher. But His best lessons weren't what He talked about, no not at all. His best lessons were taught through His example.

Jesus taught His disciples many things (thereby teaching us also as we can read about these lessons), but the one time He actually said that He was showing an example of something they should emulate was when He washed their feet. The one thing Jesus said to copy Him on was when He acted as a servant, showing love even to His enemy.

All of His other teachings draw from the truth that He showed by this act – he who wants to be first has to be last. The leader must be the servant. With that in mind, the other teachings seem to have a theme.

Jesus didn't just lecture about love, He taught it through acting it out. He went so far as to demonstrate ultimate love by dying on a cross to set captives free. That is a teacher worth learning from.

Jesus is the perfect teacher, but a dangerous view exists that sees Him as only a good teacher and not as God. To reduce Jesus to being nothing more than a good example of how to live completely does away with the very point of His incarnation, death, and resurrection.

Jesus, the heir

Hebrews 1:2 but in these last days he has spoken to us by his Son, whom he appointed the heir of all things, through whom also he created the world.

Jesus is not just a man, not an angel, not even a god. He's THE God, heir to all things, worthy of all praise and even the worship of the angels. All things have been granted to Him. Just as a firstborn son gets an inheritance, God's Son gets the inheritance of all inheritances.

A never-ending kingdom is His, and all that's in it. His throne will know no end. He upholds the universe by the word of His power. This is His role as heir. All power and authority is His. This is a mighty thing, but Jesus shares it with us.

When we become children of God through faith in Christ, we become coheirs with Him[1]. What He has, we have. Power and authority are ours in HIs name and for His will. There's nothing that isn't His and He doesn't keep it all to Himself. We have access to the kingdom of God through Jesus Christ.

---

1   (Romans 8:17)

Jesus, the mediator

1 Timothy 2:5-6 For there is one God, and there is one mediator between God and men, the man Christ Jesus, who gave himself as a ransom for all, which is the testimony given at the proper time.

In the course of human history, many attempts have been made to reach God. People have built towers to get to heaven, invented superstitions, taken part in religious practices, called on saints, and all other sorts of things that fail to bridge the gap between God and man.

The thing is, God is holy and we're sinful. We can't get into His presence in our current state. Only someone who's lived a perfect life can get to God. Because Jesus is fully God and yet lived an earthly life free from sin as a fully human man, He's the only acceptable bridge between us and God.

When we pray, our words would fall on deaf ears were it not for Jesus petitioning on our behalf. Because His righteousness has been imparted on us, God hears us when we call out to Him. We don't pray to Jesus, we pray through Him and He takes it to the Father. Without Him, we'd have no way and no chance.

Jesus, the redeemer

Colossians 1:13-14 He has delivered us from the domain of darkness and transferred us to the kingdom of his beloved Son, in whom we have redemption, the forgiveness of sins.

You and I were once under the wrath of God, helpless to free ourselves from the state we found ourselves in. We were enemies of God and we never could have done anything to appease Him. It was beyond our ability to reach out to Him.

But God, in an act of amazing grace, reached out to us. He extended His hand in peace by offering His Son to die in our place. His perfect, sinless Son became our sin and paid the price we owed. And He set us free. He redeemed us. Do you understand the term redeemer? Do you realize the weight it carries?

A redeemer is one who buys something or someone back, say out of slavery or bondage for example. An Old Testament picture of the redeemer concept is given in the book of Ruth when Boaz redeems Ruth out of her widowhood. Jesus became our Redeemer which means He purchased us at a price. Now we belong to Him. We're His. But belonging to Christ is where true freedom is found. It's in Him that we really find life.

No one can ever take us away from our Redeemer. Once Jesus has paid the price for you, you're His, once and for all. We can never lose Him and He'll never leave us.

> *"I thought I could have leaped from earth to heaven at one spring when I first saw my sins drowned in the Redeemer's blood."*
>
> *-Charles Spurgeon*

Jesus, the friend

John 15:15 No longer do I call you servants, for the servant does not know what his master is doing; but I have called you friends, for all that I have heard from my Father I have made known to you.

Can Jesus really be your friend? The Creator of the universe, your BFF? Well, it all depends really. The first thing that needs to be pointed out is that we do not get to decide if we're friends of Jesus. He chooses us, not the other way around[1].

Secondly, there are stipulations to being a friend of God. "If you do what I command you," He says[2]. With Christ we don't get a genie in a bottle who we can manipulate to get what we want. We get a loving God who cares about us but expects us to give our lives to Him.

Are you a friend of God? Is your whole life His? You don't get to take your ball and go home in this friendship if you don't like what you're hearing. If the Lord of all chose you as His friend, you're never going to be apart from Him. In good times and in bad, He's by your side. When you need Him, He's there. When you fall, He'll pick you up. And best of all, He gave His

---

1   (John 15:16)
2   (John 15:14)

life for you. There's no greater love than that[3].

> "A rule I have had for years is: to treat the Lord Jesus Christ as a personal friend. His is not a creed, a mere doctrine, but it is He Himself we have."
>
> -D.L. Moody

---

3 (John 15:13)

Jesus, the high priest

Hebrews 5:5 So also Christ did not exalt himself to be made a high priest, but was appointed by him who said to him, "You are my Son, today I have begotten you"

In the days of the Old Testament priests, a sacrifice was made on behalf of the people by the High Priest. This would atone for their sins for the period of one year. In this way the priest brought God and man together.

Jesus is the perfect High Priest because He serves as both the priest and the sacrifice. He brings God and man together by the shedding of His own blood, not that of an animal. The sacrifice of this perfect Lamb is once and for all, not just to atone for a limited period of time.

Jesus didn't appoint Himself to the position of High Priest, but He's the only one who can fill the role perfectly. Unlike all other High Priests who had to offer sacrifices for their own sins as well as those of the people, Jesus can atone for our sins by offering His own life in the place of ours. And that's just what He did.

Jesus, the perfect Adam

Romans 5:18 Therefore, as one trespass led to condemnation for all men, so one act of righteousness leads to justification and life for all men.

Adam, the first created man, was made to glorify God. In everything he did from having dominion over the earth to naming every animal created, Adam was meant to be an image-bearer of God. He was created in the image of God.

As you know, the story goes that Adam didn't succeed at being perfect, holy, or righteous. He, along with the first woman, Eve, introduced sin into the world. They changed the whole story. No longer could mankind live in harmony, in perfect communion with God. The direct link between God and man was broken.

But Jesus also bears the image of God. He wasn't created, like Adam, He's always been. But where Adam fell short , Jesus succeeded perfectly. Death came through Adam because he brought sin to humanity, but life came through Christ because He defeated sin and brought righteousness to humanity.

We needed one who had lived a perfect life free from sin to be our perfect sacrificial atonement for the forgiveness of our sins. Jesus is that one, the one perfect image-bearer of God. Because of Him, the image of God is us has been restored. He is the fulfillment of Adam's calling – the perfect Adam.

"Christ is much more powerful to save, than Adam was to destroy."

-John Calvin

Jesus, the perfect Moses

John 1:17 For the law was given through Moses; grace and truth came through Jesus Christ.

Long ago, God handed down the Law through His servant Moses. We know the Ten Commandments but many more rules and regulations were established for God's people – to show them how to be holy. If one could keep all of the Law, they could be righteous. The problem is, no one can keep all of the Law. The Law does not have the power to enable us to do what it says. It can guide, but its power ends there.

That's where Jesus comes in. He fulfills the Law because He's perfect, but He also sets us free from the Law so that we don't have to live under its burden. Because He is righteous, we can be righteous through Him instead of through keeping the Law. In Him we have forgiveness for the times we haven't kept the Law because only one who has perfectly kept it has any right to grant that forgiveness.

His grace makes us free to obey out of love instead of obligation. In fact, the more we understand His grace the more we want to obey. The Law shows us sanctification, Jesus empowers us to achieve it. He is the fulfillment of Moses' calling – the perfect Moses.

> "If Christ cannot supersede the Law, then I am lost, and lost for ever."
>
> -Catherine Booth

Jesus, the perfect Jonah

Matthew 12:41 The men of Nineveh will rise up at the judgment with this generation and condemn it, for they repented at the preaching of Jonah, and behold, something greater than Jonah is here.

The story of Jonah is one of redemption. The prophet was sent to a people that God wanted to reach with His message. Jonah's dislike of the people caused him to initially refuse the assignment. But as we know, he eventually did go and the people did receive God's message of repentance through Jonah. Despite their turning their hearts toward God, however, Jonah still refused to love these people.

Contrast this with the story of Jesus, who obediently went to the people God wanted to reach. Unlike the Ninevites, these people rejected Jesus' message and did not turn toward God. And here, unlike Jonah, Jesus chose to love them anyway. He came out of His love and He remained in His love. Then, in the ultimate act of love, He died for those who had rejected Him.

Jesus was the perfect missionary. He lived out a perfect life as an example and spoke with authority. Though the people rejected Him, He fulfilled the call of Jonah, making Him the perfect Jonah.

Jesus, the good shepherd

John 10:14-15 I am the good shepherd. I know my own and my own know me, just as the Father knows me and I know the Father; and I lay down my life for the sheep.

You don't need to know them, you just need to know Him. Many Christians spend a lot of time on learning to discern spirits so that when the time comes they'll know who it is that speaks to them. The best thing we can do though, is learn to hear the voice of Jesus.

The Good Shepherd said that those who are of His flock know His voice, that all the rest are strangers and we'll know not to listen to them. The more time spent with Jesus, the more we'll know His voice. We won't need to practice knowing other voices so as not to listen to them, we just won't listen to them because they're not Him.

Only one died for His flock. Jesus laid down His life for us, the Son of God sacrificing Himself that those who belong to Him would know life. He laid down His life on His own authority and He took it back up on His own authority. That's a voice worth listening to.

Jesus, the victorious one

1 Corinthians 15:57 But thanks be to God, who gives us the victory through our Lord Jesus Christ.

No matter what the scenario, Jesus wins. Sin? He conquers it. Death? He defeats it. Enemies? They stand no chance against the risen Son of God. He wins – period.

The victory of Christ translates into our own lives, though we don't always realize it and put it into practice. The enemies that we face, the trials, the temptations, the suffering – His victory bought ours. We are more than conquerers in Christ Jesus. His victory is our victory.

We can't achieve any of these victories on our own. WIthout the power of Christ we're utterly incapable and we'll never win over anything. But in Him we can't lose. If our goals are His goals and our desires are His desires, we're assured of victory.

Jesus not only wins in the end, He's already won. He's already triumphed over sin and death, already crushed the enemy in defeat. Because He won, we can win. Because of His victory, we get a prize.

Jesus, the Word of God

John 1:1 In the beginning was the Word, and the Word was with God, and the Word was God.

Before there was anything, He was there. Before the world, before time, Jesus existed as God and with God. Nothing that we know was made without Him. He had His hand in it all – and He still does.

The Word became flesh. He entered into time and put skin on for our benefit. He lived and walked among us, to complete a life lived without sin in complete righteousness. He was God's revelation of Himself to man, eating and drinking among them, feeling their pain, and laying down His own life, on His own accord.

The treasure of heaven, God's best, left and entered into His creation. He bankrupted heaven to be born a baby to a virgin mother of no wealth. The Word became a servant and showed us what love really is. Jesus was and is, in every way, God's way of showing Himself – His character, His love, His example, His sacrifice, His forgiveness. He is God.

Jesus, the light of the world

John 8:12 Again Jesus spoke to them, saying, "I am the light of the world. Whoever follows me will not walk in darkness, but will have the light of life."

"Let there be light." These words were spoken and so it all began. Time and all that exists came to be only after this one sentence brought about the beginning. And then, in the course of human history, the true Light came into the world. The one who spoke light into being was the true Light, and in Him all can be enlightened[1].

Just as we stumble around in the darkness for lack of light, we stumble around in our sin, lost in it, without the Light of the World. If we walk with Jesus, we will never walk in darkness because He will guide us. He'll be the lamp to our feet and the light to our path[2].

Also, if we walk with Jesus we'll ourselves be light to the world[3]. In us, the world will see Him. They'll find hope in Him, they'll see His love. Our lives will bear witness to the

---

1   (John 1:9)
2   (Psalm 119:105)
3   (Matthew 5:14)

One who sent us, just as His life bore witness to the One who sent Him[4].

So let His light shine through you. Others may see it and turn to Him.[4]

> "*The nearer you take anything to the light, the darker its spots will appear; and the nearer you live to God, the more you will see your own utter vileness.*"
>
> -*Robert Murray McCheyne*

---

4   (John 8:18)
4   (Matthew 5:16)

Jesus, the way

John 14:6 Jesus said to him, "I am the way, and the truth, and the life. No one comes to the Father except through me.

Today we like to think we're very enlightened, so much more educated than the ancients. We think we're bright enough to pick and choose aspects of different religions, tailoring our belief system, and we think this is some new thought. Actually, the Pagans of centuries ago saw no problem with pledging allegiance to multiple deities from different backgrounds until they found what suited them.

Jesus was clear though when He spoke of the way to God. Only He can serve as that bridge. Only through belief on Him can we see heaven. He is the only way. We can try out custom-made religions, but in the end they're empty, devoid of any true meaning. Christ has the answer.

By God's grace we're saved; we can't do anything to earn our way to Him. But He extended this grace in the offering of His Son on our behalf for the forgiveness of sins. This action by God just shows how He expects us to be reconciled to Him. Only through Jesus. And only means only.

Jesus, the truth

John 14:6 Jesus said to him, "I am the way, and the truth, and the life. No one comes to the Father except through me.

What is truth? The question has been asked through the ages. Even Pontius Pilate, with the Son of God standing before Him, posed the question. So often we're like Pilate, asking what truth is when it's standing right in front of us. Truth doesn't exist outside of God. Jesus is truth in the form of a man.

No one has ever spoken nothing but the complete truth their entire life except for Christ. No matter how hard we may try, we all speak untruth from time to time, even when it's not intentionally. But not one word that ever came from the mouth of Jesus was false. If He said it, we can believe it.

So what did He say? He said He was God[1]. He said He would rise from the dead[2]. He said He had all power and authority[3]. Now we either believe Him in all of it or we believe none of it. There is no in-between. If we say He was a good teacher but discredit Him as the Son of God, we have to look past the fact

---

1   (John 10:30)
2   (Matthew 20:19)
3   (Matthew 28:18)

that He claimed Himself to be God. If He claimed to be God but wasn't, that isn't a good teacher...that's a liar.

The source of truth is God. His goodness testifies to truth and there is only truth in Him. He can't lie[4]. If He says it, it's worth believing.

> "The gospel is not speculation but fact. It is truth, because it is the record of a Person who is the Truth."
>
> -Alexander MacLaren

---

4   (Numbers 23:19)

Jesus, the life

John 11:25-26 Jesus said to her, "I am the resurrection and the life. Whoever believes in me, though he die, yet shall he live, and everyone who lives and believes in me shall never die. Do you believe this?"

Are you dead? We all die at some point, but some of us die before others, some of us give up our lives and die while we still live. Is this confusing? We're all destined to die in our earthly bodies, bound for eternity either in heaven with God or hell apart from Him. But those who live in Christ have already died to themselves (in spirit) and taken on Christ's life. That's why we say we "live in Him". It's why Paul wrote of us dying to sin, dying to our old nature, etc. We've taken on a new life in Christ, we're "hidden in Him"[1]. Eternal life, for those who are in Christ, has already begun while still living on the earth.

Jesus said that He is the only way to God[2]. He also stated that He came to give life[3]. But the core truth behind this is that He is life and that's how He's able to offer it to us. Sin equals death, Jesus equals life. We choose one or the other, there are no other choices. Sin doesn't mean doing bad things, it means

---

1   (Colossians 3:3)
2   (John 14:6)
3   (John 10:10)

having an unrighteous nature. But following Christ brings onto us His nature and therefore we die to the sinful one.

He is the resurrection (the way to heaven), and the source of eternal life. If we're in Him, we'll never die (in the sense that those who spend eternity in hell "die" apart from Him). It all rests in Him, everything here and now and everything that comes after this. It begins with Him[3] and it ends with Him[4].

---

3 (John 1:1)
4 (Revelation 22:12-13)

Three in One – Prayer

*1 Timothy 2:5 For there is one God, and there is one mediator
between God and men, the man Christ Jesus*

*Ephesians 6:18a praying at all times in the Spirit, with all prayer
and supplication.*

One aspect of Christian belief that does not often make its way
into devotions or teaching on how to apply biblical truth to
daily living is the Triune nature of God. We neglect to focus on
the nature of God as three persons in one as part of our view of
God in daily life. But it's essential that we remember who God
is as we seek to know Him more, as we petition Him, as we
carry out His will.

As we pray, we are in fact engaging with all three distinct
persons of the Trinity. We speak to the Father, asking Him for
our needs to be met, giving Him praise, interceding for the
needs of others, and giving Him thanks. We do this through
the Son, who is our mediator. Were it not for the role of Jesus
Christ standing in the gap between man and God, we would
have no access to the throne and our prayers would go
unanswered. Since God himself is spirit, we must act in the
Holy Spirit to communicate with Him. All three persons of the

Triune God are present and active as we pray.

We can't neglect any part of God's nature as we seek Him. If we forget that He is good, we will have an unnatural fear of Him. If we forget that He is all-powerful, we will tend to pray without expecting results. If we forget that He is all-knowing, we may fear that we won't quite say the right thing and that God will answer our prayers incorrectly because we didn't get our message across right. The fact is that God is all of these things and He is present in our lives as our Father, as Jesus the Son, and as the Holy Spirit.

Three in One – Calling

Matthew 3:16-17 And when Jesus was baptized, immediately he went up from the water, and behold, the heavens were opened to him, and he saw the Spirit of God descending like a dove and coming to rest on him; and behold, a voice from heaven said, "This is my beloved Son, with whom I am well pleased."

What we see at the baptism of Jesus is the Father confirming the ministry He was sent for and the Holy Spirit empowering Him by coming upon Him. Jesus, being God himself, is at all times filled with the Holy Spirit, but the picture we get here as believers is that when God calls us to something, He empowers us to do it. We have the blessing of the Father, the authority given by the Son[1], and the indwelling of the Holy Spirit, which enables us to carry out God's mission.

All three persons of the Trinity are at work as we carry on with what God has called us to do and each plays a part in their own respective roles along the way. As finite humans who are quite incapable of fully understanding how God works, we may never know exactly how God is working in a given situation, but we can know that He is working and that He is simultaneously acting in the distinct persons of the Father, the Son, and the

---

1   (Matthew 28:18)

Holy Spirit. These three are one and He equips us to do what we're called to do.

> You don't have to be called into full time ministry as a pastor to be called into ministry. It's the calling of every Christian to make disciples.

Three in One – the necessity of the Trinity

Romans 3:22-24 the righteousness of God through faith in Jesus Christ for all who believe. For there is no distinction: for all have sinned and fall short of the glory of God, and are justified by his grace as a gift, through the redemption that is in Christ Jesus,

Some may ask, "Why is the Trinity so important to Christian belief?". Why, for instance, can't I just believe in God and leave it at that? Why do I need to know that God is Three in One? This is a valid question and it really has more than one answer.

Without the Trinity, we lose the Gospel. Man is sinful and God's wrath[1] is upon us. Jesus, the Son, comes to earth to take the sins of man upon Himself and imputes His righteousness on to those who believe on Him. This brings reconciliation with the Father. Upon His departure back to the Father's side, the Holy Spirit is given to the regenerate Christian to empower him or her to live out God's will. If we lose any part of this plan, we lose all of it. Each person of the Trinity plays His role in the redemption of man. No Trinity, no salvation and no right relationship with God.

Without the Trinity, the Bible makes little sense. Some

---

1   (The Father's)

Christians believe in something called Modalism, where God is one, but acts in different modes at different times. The Father created the world. Jesus was the manifestation of God as a man on earth. The Holy Spirit is active today in the lives of Christians. In Modalism, God does not exist as three persons simultaneously. But then, why did Jesus come to pay the price of man's sins to satisfy the wrath of God? How then did God the Father speak from heaven as Jesus was baptized and the Holy Spirit descend on Him like a dove? It's a stretch to makes sense of such things.

The reasoning goes on, but what every Christian needs to understand about the Trinity is that God is real right now in your life and is capable of acting in any capacity necessary. God our Father, Jesus our Mediator, and Holy Spirit our Helper. They are Three and they are One.

Three in One – Perfect Community

Ephesians 4:4-7 There is one body and one Spirit—just as you were called to the one hope that belongs to your call— one Lord, one faith, one baptism, one God and Father of all, who is over all and through all and in all. But grace was given to each one of us according to the measure of Christ's gift.

So how does believing in the Trinity affect your life? How do you live differently because of the triune God? What part of believing that God is made of one substance but three persons makes this doctrine "Christian" and what does it mean for the church?

While many religions around the world focus on works and performance, Christianity stands out. We, as Christ followers, don't give all of our focus to our performance, but the core of our belief is relationship. God is about relationships. In fact, the very first model of a perfect community is given in the Trinity. In the Bible we have Father, Son and Holy Spirit as an example for us of relationships.

There is no sin in God so He is not tainted by its effects. Among the Father, Son and Holy Spirit are truth, love, humility, peace, service, honor, and unity. There is no

175

grumbling or complaining, no backstabbing, no gossip. Though all three persons of the Trinity are equally God, there are different roles for each. But we never see the Son disgruntled about carrying out the will of the Father, we never see the Holy Spirit resent bringing glory to the Son. Because within each person of the Trinity there is the others (all one God, all one essence), they work together in perfect harmony.

We can't be perfect, so we can't live in the unity and harmony of God, but we have an example set before us to mimic to the best of our ability. Not to gain perfection, but to carry on good relationships, both with other people and with God. God is about community, about selfless relationships and love.

Three in One – God revealed

Deuteronomy 29:29 The secret things belong to the LORD our God, but the things that are revealed belong to us and to our children forever, that we may do all the words of this law.

Anyone who's ever tried to understand the triune nature of God knows that it's a difficult task. It's even harder to describe than it is to understand. People have attempted many different ways of describing God over the centuries and all of them fall short.

The water analogy[1] fails to capture the nature of God because H2O cannot exist as water, ice, and steam simultaneously and each of these three has different properties. God is simultaneously Father, Son and Holy Spirit. Each contains the same essence. The candle analogy[2] is even worse as each fail to coexist with each other in a way that would even come close to a picture of the Trinity. Likewise analogies like the courtroom[3] cannot capture the triune nature of God because saying that all of these make up "one court" is nothing like the oneness of our God. Analogies fall short because God is above our

---

1   (God is like water: it exists as liquid, solid and vapor)
2   (Father=candlestick, Son=light, Spirit=flame)
3   (which gives a good idea of the roles of the Trinity in judge, bailiff and defense attorney)

understanding.

We have a tendency to think that we need to figure everything out, that there is somewhere out there a perfect analogy to show just what our God is like. But God is not like anything in creation. He is God. And it's ok to not understand the mysterious things about Him. But when He reveals something about Himself, it's worth taking note.

Through the Scriptures, God has revealed that He is Three in One, and we do well to believe it to be so. All of the details of this fact may remain a mystery, and we need to be willing to accept that God is more complex than we could ever understand with our finite minds. If He wasn't, He wouldn't be much of a god.

He creates

Genesis 1:1 In the beginning, God created the heavens and the earth.

Any discussion of God the Father has to begin...in the beginning. God existed before there was time and then, He created time. This is confusing to almost anyone and we won't spend much time discussing eternity, but the basis of discussing God is the creation of time and all things in existence. Before He spoke it, it didn't exist.

Clearly, Jesus played a role in creation. Colossians and the Gospel of John make that very clear. But God the Father has the authority to speak things into existence, and so it was with the creation of the world. He spoke, and there was light. He spoke and there was night and there was day. He spoke, and His words were so powerful that whatever He said happened. Now why is it again that we question whether God is powerful enough to help us in our lives?

There was nothing but Him, and then there was what He created. That's pretty simple, yet it's so incredibly complicated. How did God exist from eternity if nothing else existed? How did creation take place? Was it a big bang? These are honestly mysteries that aren't going to be answered easily. We can never know everything about God, but we do know this, our Father set the universe in place, and all things hold together because of Him. We can rely on Him for all of our lives' issues.

Here's a challenge for today: Look at the things around you during the course of your daily activities and take note of the fact that God created all of them. Every person was designed by God, every man-made thing was something God allowed people the ability to learn. How does it change your day?

He calls

1 Corinthians 1:9 God is faithful, by whom you were called into the fellowship of his Son, Jesus Christ our Lord.

We like to make much of what we do for God and what we've done to change since becoming Christians, but we leave out how much of the work was done by God himself. Much of what we take credit for was initiated by Him and we merely carried out what He called us to do. Let's step aside for the moment and consider His calling.

God calls us into fellowship with himself through Jesus. He wants us to be His. He's a loving Father who adores us and would have us all follow Him in love. He calls us into good works. He wants to see us do something with our faith, not just believe but show our love for Him by serving others and serving Him. We're His vessels here on earth to do His will, but it requires us letting Him have control of the wheel.

He calls us to repentance. God wants us to seek after Him with a sorrow for the things we've done to keep us from Him. We can't serve sin and God, so when it comes down to it, He's calling us to genuinely give up the sin and follow Him. He calls us to holiness. We can't be perfect, but we can be in a right relationship with God through Christ. Holiness and righteousness are His in which to cloak us and we receive them when we follow Him. He calls each of us to ministry. Not all of us will leave our careers and become pastors and preachers, but we all have a ministry in which God can use us to expand His kingdom and bring glory unto himself.

He's calling even now. There's something tugging on your heart that you know you ought to do. You read something in God's Word that the Holy Spirit emphasized in your heart. You are being called and your response does not mean that you are doing anything on your own. Your answer to the call is out of obedience.

He commissions

Matthew 9:38 therefore pray earnestly to the Lord of the harvest to send out laborers into his harvest.

We're not only called by God, but we're sent by Him as well. He calls us to be what He wants us to be and He sends us to do what He would have done. God can do anything He wants in this world because He is all-powerful, but He chooses to use people to carry out His purposes in most cases. We have the privilege of bearing the commission of the Lord.

When considering what it means to be commissioned, it's important that we realize it's more than just being sent. The word commission carries with it the authorization of the sender, and even the granting of power to perform the duties one is commissioned to do. Our Lord does not just send us, He empowers us to accomplish every act and every goal. One who is commissioned acts on behalf of the one who sent them.

The one who sends us is the Most High God, the creator and sustainer of all things. He holds the universe in balance and He is more than capable of giving us what we need to succeed. If we make ourselves available to do what He calls us to do, He will send us and equip us for the task. He will look after us.

He protects

Psalm 23:4 Even though I walk through the valley of the shadow of death, I will fear no evil, for you are with me; your rod and your staff, they comfort me.

Our loving heavenly Father watches over His flock and will not lose even one without knowing about it. There's nowhere that we can go where we'll be outside His sight and His protection. He can and does protect us. We have nothing to fear.

The things of this world can be dangerous to anyone, but to a follower of Christ, some of them are downright disastrous outside the grace of God. He keeps us from harm and allows nothing to prosper against us as we carry out His purposes. If we're on the path He sets us on, we'll see plenty of opposition, but He'll be the One who keeps us going, guarding us all the way.

He know our weaknesses and won't allow us to face more temptation than we can bear. In fact, when faced with temptation, God provides us a way out! He gives us the avenue to get away from it, because He cares about our future. He has things for us to do and He'll provide a way for us to make it to the finish line. He's there for us, even when it sometimes seems He's not. He's never off duty, He's always watching over us, like a shepherd who cares about each and every one of his little sheep.

Just remember: Sometimes what we see as troubles are things God is using to work in our lives.

He provides

Matthew 6:11 Give us this day our daily bread.

We all have needs. Every one of us has something that we can't
live without, even if it's only the basics of food and water. But
no matter what our needs may be, they are supplied by our
Father in heaven. All good gifts are from above[1].

What's more, God knows what we need before we do. He's
aware of our everyday necessities and even our desires. He
provides not only what we need to survive, but to thrive and to
carry out His purposes. If He calls us to it, He'll equip us to
carry it out. We're never left without the required tools and
skills to be used by God. He's always ready to give.

Though He knows what we need, in some cases God does want
us to ask of Him what we seek. It may be at times that He gives
out of His grace and we never even knew to ask. It may,
however, be at times that He withholds something from us until
we petition Him. This is His prerogative, but it's done to keep
us aligned with His will. If we ask what He wills, it will
certainly be given.

---

1   (James 1:17)

He adopts

Galatians 4:6 But when the fullness of time had come, God sent forth his Son, born of woman, born under the law, to redeem those who were under the law, so that we might receive adoption as sons.

Christian, you have been chosen. Just as an adopted child is chosen by his parents, so too have you been chosen by God and given all the rights due one of His children. Women shouldn't be put off by the masculine language here. It's good that we're all called "sons" of God, despite our gender, because the firstborn son in any first century family who would have been reading this letter written by Paul would have had an abundance of rights that the other children would not have had. We should all be pleased to be called sons of God.

He has adopted us into His family through His Son, Jesus Christ. Through Jesus' life, death on the cross, and resurrection from the dead, God sent an invitation to us to be part of the family. When we respond, the adoption is final and we gain child status. The adopted children of God have rights to everything the firstborn has as co-heirs with Christ[1].

Not everyone is a child of God, though He created everyone.

---

1   (Romans 8:17)

Only those who belong to Him through faith in Jesus Christ are His adopted children. But if you are His, take comfort in the knowledge that He chose you to be part of His family. Even while you were still just a sinner, He chose you and called you to Himself. He loves you that much.

He disciplines

Hebrews 12:7-8 It is for discipline that you have to endure. God is treating you as sons. For what son is there whom his father does not discipline? If you are left without discipline, in which all have participated, then you are illegitimate children and not sons.

How does a child learn to do what's right? They learn through the example their parents give, yes, but they also learn through correction and discipline when they do the wrong things. By being taught what the rights things are and disciplined over the wrong things, a child can grow into maturity, knowing right from wrong.

How does a Christian learn what God wants? We have Jesus as our example and we have the commandments to guide us in what's right. But when we stray from what God has taught us doesn't He also correct us? Doesn't He sometimes put us back on the right track because He loves us? There's a big difference between punishment and discipline. Some have the view that God is up above watching for us to mess up so He can take His vengeance on us. That action out of anger would be punishment. But God doesn't punish those He loves. He disciplines them.

The truth is, we may not always even know we're being disciplined. The Father may remove something from us that isn't good for us in a way that provides correction. We may not even have been aware of what happened. God may also put people in our lives at certain times that give some correction. Whatever the method, God disciplines because He loves. Any parent who provides no guidance and no boundaries to their children does not love them. If a child is allowed to destroy themselves, the parent has no love for them. But our Father does love us, and He loves us enough to make sure we're everything we're supposed to be.

He shapes

Isaiah 64:8 But now, O Lord, you are our Father; we are the clay; and you are our potter; we are all the work of your hand.

What does God want from us? Sometimes we need but ask Him. We'll find many times that He's already at work in us to bring about His purposes. We are His instruments in this life, if we've given ourselves over to Him...and really even if we haven't[1]. He makes us into what He needs us to be, what He wants us to be.

We all have our own desires and our own ideas about what being godly means, but it's God himself who determines what our strengths and weaknesses are, what our opportunities will be, what our roles in life will be. But we get to where we are in His great plan one step at a time, one little minor change at a time. We experience and encounter things that develop us as a people and then we in turn become a little bit more of what God intended. If we're following Christ, we'll be used for good. God will have us play out a role on His team. The wicked and ungodly play a role too in His plan, but not for the same side.

---

1   (Romans 9:20-23)

Pray for wisdom, pray that God the Father would work on you to make you into the creation He intended you to be. Seek to be more like Christ, in His character and in His devotion to the Father. Let God work in you and through you as He shapes you into a fine piece of art.

It's hard to pray for God to send us hardship so that we'll grow. How can we take a good outlook toward this kind of growth that will cause us to pray gladly?

He judges

Isaiah 33:22 For the Lord is our judge; the Lord is our lawgiver; the Lord is our king; he will save us.

The bad news is, God is our judge. His standard for "good" is perfection. We can never live up to the requirements for being judged "not guilty". The good news is, the Judge is on our side.

If we're in Christ, we have a mediator who acts on our behalf to keep the Judge's wrath from us. The Judge sees His Son in us and rules in our favor.

Which of us is worthy of judging another? We've all committed sins and are guilty of our own transgressions. How could we judge anyone with so many strikes against us? But God isn't like us. The Judge is without sin, without blemish. He is holy, and only one who is holy is worthy to judge. He alone holds the right to hand down a verdict.

One day we'll all stand before Him and He'll make His ruling. We're either not-guilty because we've believed on Christ for our salvation, or we're guilty because we tried to be good enough on our own and didn't measure up. Where will you stand on the final judgement day? Will you be acquitted of all charges because Christ your mediator stands between you and the Judge, or will you find yourself accused without counsel to defend you?

Belief in the triune nature of God is essential to understanding the Father's role as Judge. If there are not three distinct persons that make up the Godhead, there can be no appeasement of wrath through Jesus' sacrificial death, and in that case, there's no need for a Holy Spirit in our lives.

He loves

John 3:16 For God so loved the world, that he gave his only Son, that whoever believes in him should not perish but have eternal life.

God isn't just another person in life who goes around saying things He doesn't mean. God cannot lie and He does not make promises He doesn't keep. When He says He loves us, He doesn't just leave it at that. He demonstrates it.

Do we understand what it means that God loves us? Do we grasp the heaviness of the fact that the one who created all things has affection for us? That He thinks about us? That He has a plan for us? He works in our lives, shaping us to be who He created us to be. He disciplines us when we've done wrong, just as a father disciplines his children so that they'll learn right from wrong. God shows His love by being involved in our lives.

In an act that could never be confused for anything but love, God sent His Son to die a painful death of suffering on a cross, taking on our sin and giving us His righteousness, so that He could have a relationship with us. This act was not because we had done anything to earn His love, but because He just loved us that much.

When we struggle in life, when things just don't seem to make sense, when we feel like no one loves us, we can look at all that God has done for us. Look to the forgiveness you've received in Christ, to the wonderful promises God has made, and to the Holy Spirit He's placed in your life to comfort and guide you. He loves you so much that He can't stay away from you. He's crazy about you.

Most people have John 3:16 memorized, whether they're a Christian or not. I challenge you to read this verse in full context and try to memorize verses 17 and 18 in addition to what you already know.

The Church

Hebrews 10:24-25 And let us consider how to stir up one another to love and good works, not neglecting to meet together, as is the habit of some, but encouraging one another, and all the more as you see the Day drawing near.

Sometimes it's hard to know where we belong in this world. We can find ourselves tossed aside by society if we're not pretty enough or cool enough for the world's standards. We have to meet the criteria of whatever group we're looking to be accepted by in order to have a shot. But in God's family, there's always room for the outcast or the downtrodden.

In fact, sometimes it takes feeling the rejection of the world for us to turn to God, and when we do, we find a Father who has His arms open wide. There are many churches and many denominations and it's not accurate to say that all of them are as accepting as Christ is, but in general the church is where we find a home where His love is shown. The fellowship of believers is where we can find the love, encouragement, motivation, kindness, and correction the world lacks. Each believer is equipped to minister to others in some way, and everyone has a place where they fit in.

God's overall plan is fulfilled through His Church (outwardly) and the body is meant to minister to each other (inwardly) for this plan to be accomplished. Our mission isn't just to go "out there", but also to tend to those "in here" so that each of us can be better at what we're called to do. Healing, hope, and love are found in Christ's Church. This was His plan.

Hoping for something more

Luke 24:21a But we had hoped that he was the one to redeem Israel...

Have you ever looked back on something in your life and realized how foolish you looked for not seeing what was right in front of you? The story in Luke's account of the Gospel about two disciples who were talking while they traveled, just days after Jesus' death on the cross, makes one wonder just how foolish they felt as they looked back at their encounter with Jesus.

As they walked along sulking that this man they had followed, who that had placed their trust in as the promised Messiah, the one who would redeem His people Israel, the resurrected Jesus actually joined them. These two of His disciples recounted the story of Jesus' crucifixion to Him[1] and expressed lament over the fact that He hadn't lived up to their hopes.

We look back now and wonder how on earth the risen Lord could have disappointed anyone's hopes, but these Jewish men had been awaiting a Messiah who would establish an earthly kingdom to save them from their oppressors and Jesus did not

---

1   (because they didn't recognize Him as being Jesus)

do that. No, instead He was killed by those oppressors. This fell short of what they had wanted from Him.

But Jesus came to do so much more than just save Israel from an oppressive government. He came to bring reconciliation with God, to all, Jews and Gentiles alike. But the men didn't know this yet because they were so focused on their own expectations. Can't we do that sometimes? Don't we sometimes expect God to answer us in some small way and when we don't see it we get all upset with Him, when really there's a much bigger blessing in store if we'd only open our eyes? The guys in this story opened their eyes and eventually saw Jesus for who He was and what He came to do. That's hope for all of us.

Head knowledge and heart knowledge

Luke 24:25 And he said to them, "O foolish ones, and slow of heart to believe all that the prophets have spoken!

Our friends who encountered Jesus along the road to Emmaus days after His death on the cross were very knowledgeable of the Scriptures. They longed for the promised Jewish Messiah because they had been taught from a young age all about the manuscripts and the Law, the oral traditions and the customs. They knew the stories of their ancestors inside and out. But Jesus pointed out to them that their head knowledge did not equal knowing the Scripture in their hearts.

He rightly pointed out to the disciples that they were being foolish for knowing the promises of God through the prophets without realizing that they were being fulfilled right in front of their eyes — by the very man who stood before them! They were so concerned with what they "knew" that they didn't know anything. They couldn't see the forrest for the trees. All of that teaching did them no good if they couldn't recognize the One whom the prophets had foretold.

Before we get down on the poor disciples of this story let's take a look at the modern day church, at ourselves. We're a very educated society, with so many schools and so much at our disposal for learning about God and His Word. Many of us have quite a few verses memorized and have learned the stories of the Bible from a young age. We could tell someone who asks almost anything about any story...but how do those stories apply to our lives? Do we know that answer?

"Knowing" the Scriptures is not the same as seeing Jesus for who He is and what He's done by seeking Him. Knowing God on a personal level enables us to really know the Scriptures and see them with eyes wide open. Jesus has enabled us to know Him if we'll just seek Him out. If we look for Him, we'll see that the entirety of God's Word is about Jesus. From Genesis to Revelation.

Jesus in the Scriptures

Luke 24:27 And beginning with Moses and all the Prophets, he interpreted to them in all the Scriptures the things concerning himself.

Can you see Jesus? There He is, in the Garden of Eden, as the serpent is cursed by God and promised that One would come who would crush him[1]. He's there as Shadrach, Meshach, and Abednego stand among the flames without being burnt up[2]. He's the one foretold by the prophets[3] and ushered in by The Baptist[4]. And yes, we find that even in the very beginning, He was there[5]. But so much more than these examples, He's the central character of every story in every book of God's Word.

As the disciples who walked to Emmaus spoke to Jesus, He pointed out to them how all of the Scriptures they knew concerned Him, they all had a purpose of shedding light on the man who was also God. God revealed Himself to mankind through Jesus and He revealed Jesus through the Scriptures.

---

1   (Genesis 3:15)
2   (Daniel 3:24-25)
3   (2 Samuel 7:12–16; Isaiah 7:14; 9:6; 50:6; 52:13–53:12; 61:1; Jeremiah 23:5, 6; Daniel 7:13, 14; 9:24–27; Micah 5:2; Zechariah 6:12; 9:9;12:10; 13:7 and so on)
4   (John 1:29)
5   (John 1:1)

When the eyes of the disciples were opened, they saw it. When our eyes are opened to who Jesus is, we see it too. It's all about Him, every story, every prophesy, even the Law is given to show that we needed Jesus to come[1]. It's genius, if you think about it. Who else, ever, in the entire history of the world, has written such an extensive story with so much action, so much rich dialogue, such beautiful poetry, such love, such applicable moral teaching, that reveals in the end to be about a great Hero that was the basis for the rest of the story up to that point? It's brilliant! And it's God-inspired.

What the disciples got that day is that Jesus is the central character. He's the one that matters in the big scheme of things. We can learn a lot from Moses, David, Solomon and other heroes, but their main purpose was to point to Christ. Their good deeds and their flaws alike were to show us Jesus. The prophesies, the plagues, the desert wandering, the flooding, all to point us to Jesus. Not every view of theology agrees with this notion, but what matters is that Jesus did. He's the one who said Moses wrote about Him[2] and made claim to be the One that the prophets spoke of[3]. If Jesus believed it, it's best to follow His lead.

---

1   (Galatians 3:24-25)
2   (John 5:46)
3   (Luke 4:21)

The invitation

Luke 24:29 but they urged him strongly, saying, "Stay with us, for it is toward evening and the day is now far spent." So he went in to stay with them.

On the road to Emmaus, the disciples didn't see Jesus for who He was. Even after He had opened up the Scriptures to them as an ongoing story concerning Himself, they didn't realize who was in their presence. They were intrigued, maybe even amazed by His brilliance, but they did not yet see Him as the Christ because their eyes were still closed.

As they came upon their destination, Jesus acted like He was going to keep walking (knowing full well what was going to happen). The disciples invited Him to come along with them. They wanted to know more. They wanted to spend more time with this man. Only after this invitation were their eyes opened. All that they knew in their heads became real finally when it hit them that they were talking with the Christ all that time on the road. He became more than they had ever expected.

The journey of a disciple requires an invitation to Jesus. This doesn't mean salvation, because He does the inviting in our hearts and we respond. This is an invitation for Him to join us along the road as we travel into spiritual maturity. We can't understand it all on our own, we need Him walking with us. As the disciples headed to Emmaus saw, Jesus is more than willing to accept and open up our eyes.

Burning hearts

Luke 24:32 They said to each other, "Did not our hearts burn within us while he talked to us on the road, while he opened to us the Scriptures?"

The Word of God has an effect on all who experience it. As Jesus walked with the disciples that were headed to Emmaus, He opened up the Scriptures to them in a very real way, showing them the overall theme of the Bible – Himself. As they heard all of this, presumably for the first time[1], their hearts burned within them. After inviting Jesus to stay with them their eyes were opened and they saw clearly who He was and that God had revealed Himself, through Jesus and through the Scriptures.

And what happened immediately after that? The result was exactly what it was for anyone whose heart burns from within – they had to go share what they now knew. When your heart is burning, you can't help but tell the world what made it so. After hearing Jesus' words, experiencing Him, and having their eyes opened to the truth, they immediately went out and spread the news that the Christ had risen. There was no doubt left in their minds that it was true and that everyone needed to

---

1   (though they "knew" the Scriptures)

know. They knew the value of this news. They knew what it meant to all mankind.

Experiencing Jesus does this to a person. He has such an impact on us that our hearts burn from within and we can't help but share the Gospel with all of those around us. No one has ever had such an effect on all the world. Those who experienced Him for who He is turned the world upside down[1] and we can continue to do so for His glory.

> "And He departed from our sight that we might return to our heart, and there find Him. For He departed, and behold, He is here."
>
> *-Augustine*

---

1   (Acts 17:6)

About the author:

Photo by Darin Crofton Photography
http://www.darincroftonphotography.com/

Matt Cochran's passion is seeing people's lives transformed by a relationship with Jesus Christ. At Christ Fellowship of Tampa, Matt helps people take the Next Steps in their spiritual journey. With his daily devotions at devotionsfordisciples.com, he offers a guide in that journey.

Having served in the Marine Corps in locations all over the world, Matt easily connects with people. He holds a Bachelor's Degree in Christian Studies and is working on a Master's Degree in Discipleship Ministries at the time of this book's publishing. Matt is married to the love of his life, Rose, and they have two sons, Colin and Hank.

Made in the USA
Charleston, SC
23 September 2011